SAM NOIR™

Volume One

Written by
Eric A. Anderson
and Manny Trembley

Art by
Manny Trembley

Lettered by
Eric A. Anderson

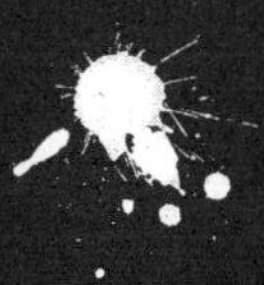

Editor
Kristen Simon

President
Jim Valentino

A

Production

some fonts provided by Blambot.com

Dedications:

For Angela, whom I would slay hundreds of ninjas to avenge, should she ever get killed by throwing stars.

-Eric

For Lisa. Without you I would not have the courage to eat an entire bag of State Fair Brand cinnamon sugar mini donuts.

-Manny

Chapter One

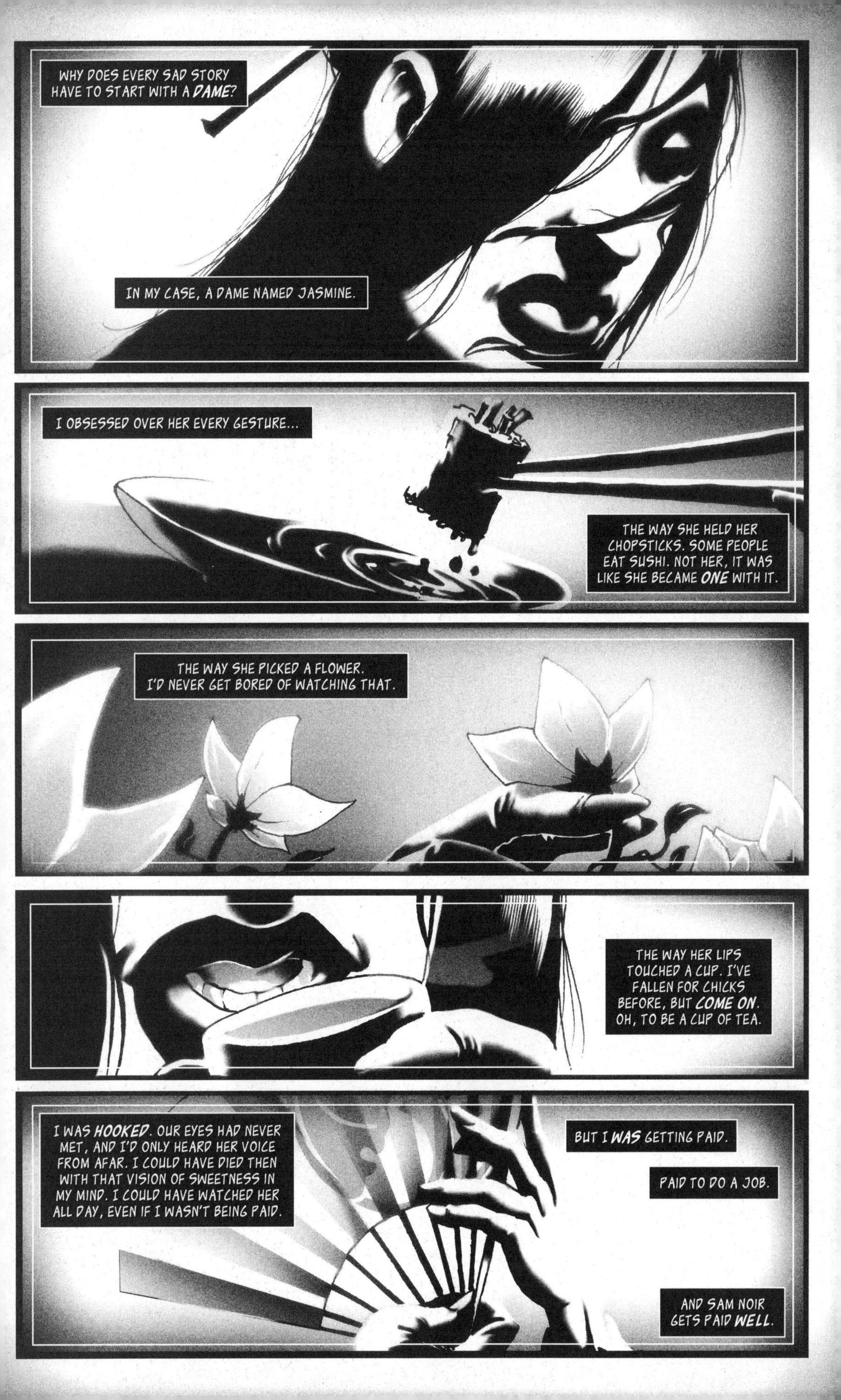
WHY DOES EVERY SAD STORY HAVE TO START WITH A **DAME**?
IN MY CASE, A DAME NAMED JASMINE.
I OBSESSED OVER HER EVERY GESTURE...
THE WAY SHE HELD HER CHOPSTICKS. SOME PEOPLE EAT SUSHI. NOT HER, IT WAS LIKE SHE BECAME **ONE** WITH IT.
THE WAY SHE PICKED A FLOWER. I'D NEVER GET BORED OF WATCHING THAT.
THE WAY HER LIPS TOUCHED A CUP. I'VE FALLEN FOR CHICKS BEFORE, BUT **COME ON**. OH, TO BE A CUP OF TEA.
I WAS **HOOKED**. OUR EYES HAD NEVER MET, AND I'D ONLY HEARD HER VOICE FROM AFAR. I COULD HAVE DIED THEN WITH THAT VISION OF SWEETNESS IN MY MIND. I COULD HAVE WATCHED HER ALL DAY, EVEN IF I WASN'T BEING PAID.
BUT I **WAS** GETTING PAID.
PAID TO DO A JOB.
AND SAM NOIR GETS PAID **WELL**.

HER NAME WAS A BEAUTIFUL WORD. SURE, I HATED THE FLOWERS SHE WAS NAMED AFTER, BUT I WOULD'VE EATEN A BUSHEL OF JASMINE FLOWERS JUST FOR HER. THEN I'D HAVE ASKED FOR SECONDS.
I DON'T TAKE JUST ANY JOB. I ONLY TAKE JOBS THAT PAY. OR ONES THAT ARE FUN TO DO... THE ONES WHERE I GET TO KILL SOMETHING.
THE JOB CAME MY WAY THROUGH THE NORMAL CHANNELS. SOMEONE ASKED ME. KEEP MY DISTANCE, THEY SAID. NO CONTACT. OBSERVATION ONLY. I CAN DO THAT.
DAYS WENT BY AND SOON THOSE DAYS BECAME MONTHS. THOSE WERE THE BEST MONTHS OF MY SORRY LIFE.
I HAD BEEN HIRED BY PEOPLE TO WATCH PEOPLE BEFORE. THE FIRST PEOPLE ALWAYS WANT YOU TO GET CLOSE TO THE SECOND PEOPLE, BUT NOT TOO CLOSE... BUT CLOSE ENOUGH TO SEE, SEE?
WHO WERE THESE PEOPLE WHO WANTED THIS PARTICULAR PERSON WATCHED? WHY DID THEY CARE SO MUCH ABOUT HOW JASMINE SPENT HER DAYS? AT THE TIME, I DIDN'T KNOW, AND I DIDN'T CARE.
I JUST DID WHAT I DO. I'M A DETECTIVE. I DETECT THINGS.

I WAS A GHOST.
I WAS HER SHADOW. BUT EVEN A SHADOW CAN FALL IN LOVE.
SOME DAYS, I WANTED HER TO TURN AROUND AND SEE ME.
SOME DAYS I WANTED TO SHOUT OUT TO HER. TELL HER TO RUN...
RUN TO ME.
BUT I KEPT MY NOSE TO THE PAVEMENT. SAM NOIR IS THE BEST DICK ON THE BEAT, AND HE STICKS TO THE PLAN.
PROBLEM IS... SOMETIMES THE PLAN DON'T STICK TO SAM.
PLANS ARE LIKE RICE PAPER. GOOD FOR BLOCKING SUNLIGHT. BUT APPLY A BIT OF PRESSURE AND YOU RIP RIGHT THROUGH IT.
SHE APPLIED THE PRESSURE.
HOW? SHE LOOKED RIGHT AT ME. NO, RIGHT THROUGH ME.
RIGHT THEN, I KNEW I'D GOTTEN TOO CLOSE. I'D LET MY GUARD DOWN.

IT WAS THE MIDDLE OF THE NIGHT, AND I COULDN'T SLEEP. FOOD DIDN'T TASTE THE SAME ANYMORE. SLEEP DIDN'T FEEL THE SAME ANYMORE. HOW COULD I FEEL THIS WAY? I DIDN'T KNOW HER. I WRESTLED WITH THAT EVERY NIGHT.
PAR FOR THE COURSE.
I'D LONG SINCE GIVEN UP THE OLD WAYS. MASTER-LESS SAMURAI DON'T HAVE ANYTHING TO GO HOME TO. AS A LITTLE BOY, ALL I WANTED WAS TO SWING A KATANA LIKE A REAL MAN. LIVE AND DIE BY THE CODE. I TRIED THE RONIN-FOR-HIRE BIT. WASN'T MY CUP O' TEA. WHY GO FIND WORK WHEN WORK WILL COME TO YOU? I MOVED TO THE CITY. I TOOK TO LIVIN' A LIFE AS A DETECTIVE. CHOOSE YOUR OWN HOURS AND DAMES IN DISTRESS...WELL, NOTHING HOTTER THAN THAT.
I CHOSE THIS RACKET FOR THE LIFESTYLE. BE YOUR OWN BOSS. MAKE YOUR OWN RULES... THAT SORT OF THING.
WHAT THEY DON'T TELL YOU IN THE BROCHURE IS THAT IT'S LONELY AS HELL OUT THERE ON THE EDGE.
THAT NIGHT, JASMINE WEIGHED ON MY MIND LIKE A BLOCK OF CEMENT... DRAGGING ME TO THE BOTTOM OF A MUDDY RIVER OF SAPPORO AND UNFILTERED MAY BLOSSOMS.
"I LOVE YOU JASMINE." CRAP. THAT SOUNDS SO PATHETIC.
THESE FIVE WORDS I SWEAR TO YOU: "I'LL BE THERE FOR YOU, DOLLFACE."
WAIT. THAT WAS 6 WORDS.
AS IF MY THOUGHTS AWOKE THE GODS AND SPAT OUT MY WISH ONTO MY OFFICE FLOOR. JASMINE WAS THERE.
MY DREAM WAS STANDING RIGHT IN FRONT OF ME. I WAS TONGUE TIED. I COULD'VE TIED MY TONGUE WITH HERS, THAT'S FOR SURE.

HER KIMONO DRAPED DOWN TO HER GETAS. HER BLEACH WHITE STOCKING FEET WERE LIKE TWO TASTY RICE BOWLS. I COULDA NIBBLED THE GRAINS ALL NIGHT.
MY CHEST FELT LIKE SOMEONE HAD STUFFED IT FULL OF DYNAMITE. MY MOUTH WENT DRY. DRY LIKE A COTTON BALL IN THE SAHARA.
MY GREATEST FEAR WAS UPON ME. THE SIREN SPOKE.
GOOD MORNING, KIND SIR.
2 AM MIGHT BE MORNING IN HER BOOK, BUT THIS WAS ALL WRONG. SHE SHOULDN'T HAVE BEEN THERE. SCREW PROTOCOL. I WANTED TO LEAP FROM MY CHAIR AND HOLD HER. I KEPT MY COOL. I ALWAYS KEEP MY COOL.
MY FAMILY NEEDS YOU.
SHE SHOULDN'T EVEN KNOW WHO I AM. SURE, OUR EYES CAUGHT ONCE. SURE, I'D FOLLOWED HER FROM ONE END OF THE CITY TO THE OTHER OVER THE COURSE OF 3 MONTHS, BUT SHE SHOULDN'T KNOW ME. I WAS IN TOO DEEP NOW. I HAD BOTCHED THE JOB.
I NEED YOU, SAM.
SHE KNEW MY NAME! THE DYNAMITE EXPLODED. THE COTTON IN MY MOUTH HAD TURNED TO DUST AND WAS CHOKING ME SILENT. AND JUST LIKE THAT, I QUIT CARING ABOUT THE JOB.
I NEEDED HER. I NEEDED HER TO NEED ME. NO... THAT DOESN'T SAY IT.. I NEEDED TO KNOW THAT SHE NEEDED ME TO NEED HER.

I'M SCARED... I...
SHE WAS SCARED ALL RIGHT... BUT OF WHAT SHE NEVER GOT THE CHANCE TO TELL ME. HER DELICATE FLOWER OF A LIFE WAS SNUFFED OUT IN A MOMENT. I'D NEVER EVEN SAID ONE WORD TO HER.
YOU PICTURE THE PERSON YOU WANT TO GROW OLD WITH, AND YOU IMAGINE YOURSELVES DYING TOGETHER IN EACH OTHERS ARMS AT A RIPE OLD AGE AND THEN, IN AN INSTANT, THAT BRIGHT FUTURE IS STRIPPED AWAY.
JASMINE TOOK THREE THROWING STARS IN THE BACK THAT NIGHT.
UH...
HER BLOOD FILLED THE CRACKS IN THE FLOORBOARDS. I'VE SPILT A LOT OF BLOOD. I MEAN A LOT. A LOT OF BLOOD ON A LOT OF WOOD FLOORS. BUT SEEING HER BLOOD, ON MY FLOOR IN MY OFFICE WITHOUT ME SPILLING IT, MADE ME SICK. I WANTED THAT TIME BACK. THEN A WHISPER LEFT HER SOFT LIPS.
SAM...
THEY SAY THROWING STARS DON'T KILL.
TELL THAT TO HER.
GOOD THING SHE DIED QUICK, BECAUSE IF I STILL HAD ANY TEARS LEFT TO GIVE, SHE WOULD HAVE DROWNED IN THAT ROOM. I'VE ONLY CRIED TWICE. ONCE WHEN MY FATHER BEAT ME FOR TOUCHING HIS KATANA AND AGAIN WHEN YUKI TURNED ME DOWN WHEN I ASKED HER TO THE SPRING FORMAL. I DON'T CRY ANYMORE.

MAYBE I SHOULDN'T HAVE LEFT HER THERE. HAD I KNOWN THAT THE LAST SEMBLANCE OF INNOCENCE IN MY LIFE WAS LAID OUT ON THAT FLOOR, MAYBE I WOULD'VE DONE THINGS DIFFERENTLY. MAYBE I WOULD'VE ALLOWED MYSELF TO MOURN HER.

MAYBE I WOULD'VE BURIED HER ***PROPER***-LIKE.

BUT I WAS ANGRY. I HAD TO KNOW WHY. I 'M A DETECTIVE. A MURDER GOES DOWN IN MY OFFICE AND I NEED TO KNOW WHO'S RESPONSIBLE.

MAYBE THINGS WOULD BE DIFFERENT IF I DIDN'T LEAP OUT THAT WINDOW. MAYBE IF I HAD KNOWN THEN WHAT I KNOW I KNOW NOW, I WOULD HAVE JUST STAYED THERE... BECAUSE, LET'S FACE IT, IGNORANCE IS ***BLISS***.

BUT I WAS A ***SAMURAI DETECTIVE***. I ***STILL*** AM. I DON'T SECOND GUESS MY CHOICES. I WALK THE HARD LINE. I HAD TO ***KNOW***, SO I LEFT HER THERE.

RIGHTS AND WRONGS. WHO CAN KNOW WHAT'S WHAT IN THIS CRAZY MIXED UP WORLD. AM I ***WRONG*** FOR WANTING TO RIGHT THE WRONG WRONGED TO JASMINE? OR AM I ***RIGHT*** FOR WANTING TO RIGHT THE WRONG WRONGED TO MY LOVE, MY LADY...MY ***FLOWER***.

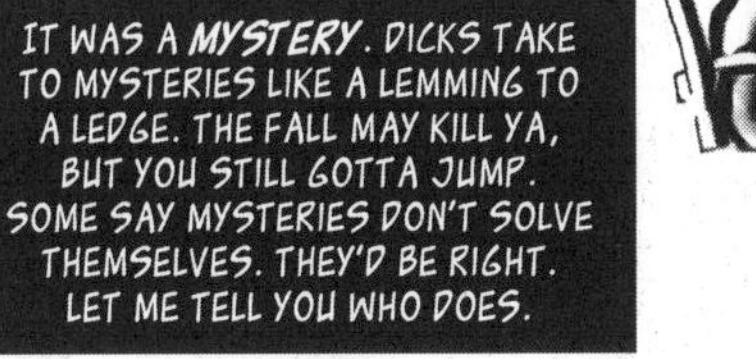

ME. THAT'S WHO.

SAM NOIR.

NOBODY EVER EXPECTS A FELLA TO JUMP OUT OF HIS THIRD STORY WINDOW. PEOPLE SHOULD EXPECT THOSE TYPES OF THINGS. I DO.
THAT'S WHY I JUMP OUT WINDOWS.
CUZ' NOBODY THINKS OF IT.
BUT THEN AGAIN...
HIRED GOONS AREN'T KNOWN FOR THEIR DEDUCTIVE REASONING.
THUGS, GOONS, NINJAS, WHATEVER. THEY'RE ALL THE SAME.
IDIOTS WITH SWORDS AND STARS. FLINGIN' THEM AT DAMES WHO DON'T DESERVE IT.
THOSE HATCHETMEN WOULD PAY FOR KILLING MY JASMINE.

YOU'RE GOING TO PAY FOR KILLIN' MY GIRL.
IT WILL BE YOU THAT PAYS, RONIN!
WITH YOUR BLOOD!
AT LEAST I STILL HAVE MY HONOR, NINJA.
WHICH OF YOU TWO MEATHEADS WANTS TO TELL ME WHO SENT YOU?
WE WILL NEVER TALK!!
IT WAS A RHETORICAL QUESTION.

THE BEST PART ABOUT THUGS IS HOW PREDICTABLE THEY ARE.
BLEED FOR HER, COWARD.
BAIT AND SWITCH. I PREFER "BLOCK AND STAB". IT'S JUST MY STYLE.
EVERYONE KNOWS STABBING COMES AFTER BLOCKING. 'CEPT HIM.
I GUESS YOU'RE THE LUCKY BUM.
HE WAS SCARED. SCARED CHUMPS ALWAYS SQUEAL.

WHY HER!? WHY MY JASMINE? SHE WAS INNOCENT.
WHO SENT YOU?
I NEVER MET HIM. ALL I HAVE IS A NAME...
MASTER FUYU.
FUYU? NEVER HEARD OF THE GUY. WHY'D HE PUT A HIT ON THE GIRL?
WE DON'T QUESTION THE MASTER'S WISHES. HE WANTED HER DEAD.
GUESS WHAT: YOU GET TO JOIN HER.
RONIN, WAIT! I'VE TOLD YOU ALL I KNOW. PLEASE LET ME LIVE!
SURE, KID. I'LL LET YOU LIVE.
JUST AS SOON AS YOU BRING BACK JASMINE.

MASTER FUYU.
THAT NAME WAS OLD-COUNTRY.
AND I HAD SOLVED PLENTY OF OTHER CASES WITH LESS INFORMATION THAN A NAME.
IT HAD BEEN ABOUT TEN YEARS SINCE I LAST WALKED THAT PATH, BUT IN REVERSE.
I PROMISED MYSELF I'D NEVER GO BACK, BUT I DIDN'T COUNT ON MY HEART GETTING BROKEN AGAIN BY YET ANOTHER DEAD GIRL.
WHERE I GREW UP, SOME KIDS - THE STUPID ONES - WANTED TO BE RICE FARMERS. SOME WANTED TO BE SWORD SMITHS.
ME, I JUST WANTED TO WHACK PEOPLE WITH A STICK.

SMACKIN' OTHERS WITH A STICK GIVES A KID A RUSH LIKE NOTHING ELSE.
THEY SAY IT TAKES A STRONG HAND TO STEER KIDS.
IF THEY MEANT A STRONG HAND ATTACHED TO A MASTER SWORDSMAN, THEY'D BE RIGHT.
I DEDICATED MY LIFE TO THE ***BUSHIDO CODE***. I DRANK IT UP LIKE SAKE.
WARM TO THE TOUCH AND NEVER DISAPPOINTING.

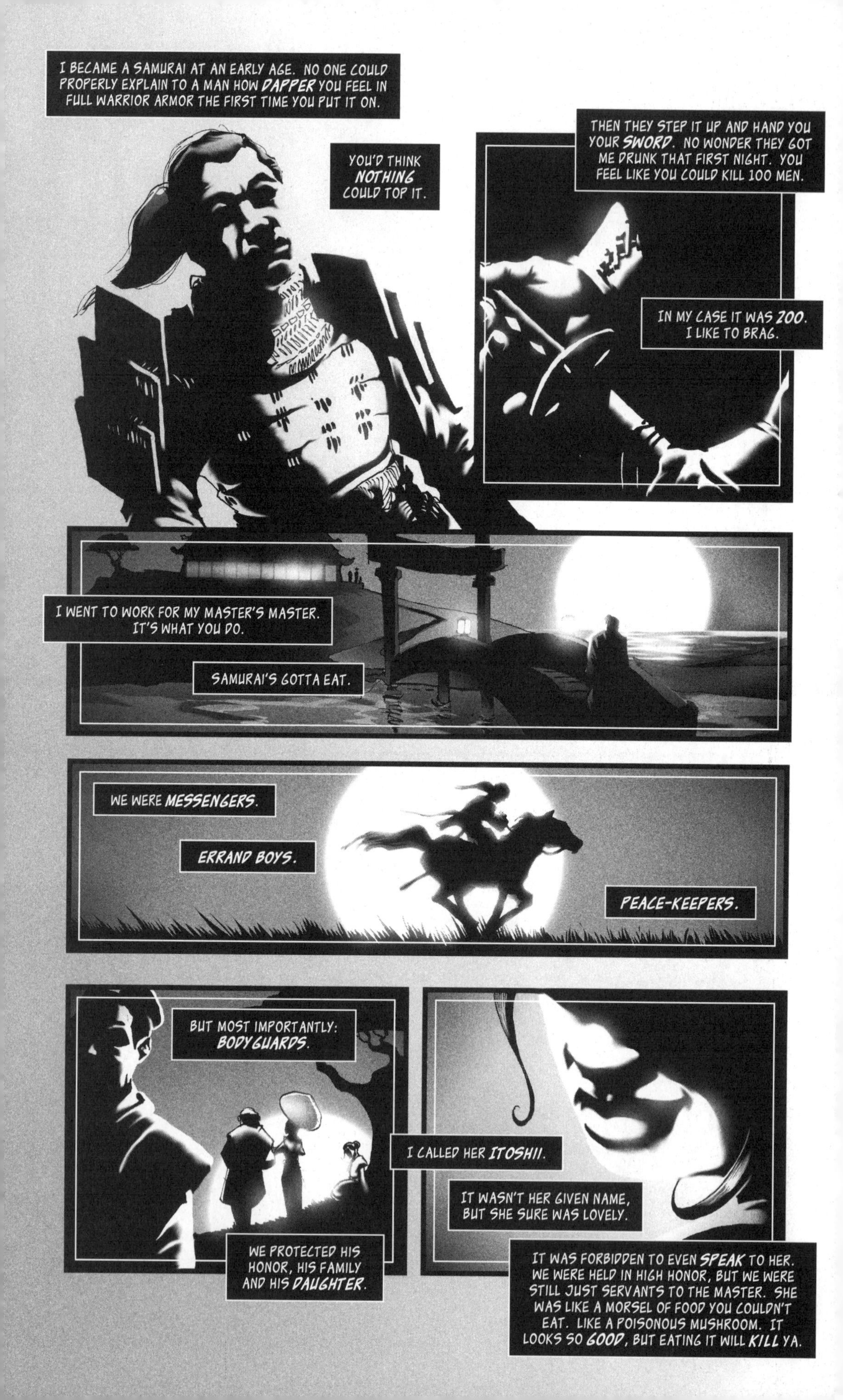
I BECAME A SAMURAI AT AN EARLY AGE. NO ONE COULD PROPERLY EXPLAIN TO A MAN HOW DAPPER YOU FEEL IN FULL WARRIOR ARMOR THE FIRST TIME YOU PUT IT ON.
YOU'D THINK NOTHING COULD TOP IT.
THEN THEY STEP IT UP AND HAND YOU YOUR SWORD. NO WONDER THEY GOT ME DRUNK THAT FIRST NIGHT. YOU FEEL LIKE YOU COULD KILL 100 MEN.
IN MY CASE IT WAS 200. I LIKE TO BRAG.
I WENT TO WORK FOR MY MASTER'S MASTER. IT'S WHAT YOU DO.
SAMURAI'S GOTTA EAT.
WE WERE MESSENGERS.
ERRAND BOYS.
PEACE-KEEPERS.
BUT MOST IMPORTANTLY: BODYGUARDS.
WE PROTECTED HIS HONOR, HIS FAMILY AND HIS DAUGHTER.
I CALLED HER ITOSHII.
IT WASN'T HER GIVEN NAME, BUT SHE SURE WAS LOVELY.
IT WAS FORBIDDEN TO EVEN SPEAK TO HER. WE WERE HELD IN HIGH HONOR, BUT WE WERE STILL JUST SERVANTS TO THE MASTER. SHE WAS LIKE A MORSEL OF FOOD YOU COULDN'T EAT. LIKE A POISONOUS MUSHROOM. IT LOOKS SO GOOD, BUT EATING IT WILL KILL YA.

SHE WAS THE ONLY OTHER DAME IN MY LIFE I'VE FALLEN FOR.
I DID TOUCH HER HAND ONCE. IT WAS ELECTRIC. LIKE A LIGHTNING BOLT. OR AN EEL.
ONE OF THEM ELECTRIC EELS.
TRAGEDY IS NEVER FAR BEHIND WHEN CHICKS ARE INVOLVED.
WE NEVER SPOKE. STANDARD FARE FOR A MOOK LIKE ME.
THE LAST IMAGE I STILL HAVE IS OF HER BURNING ALIVE WITH HER FAMILY.
IT WAS ONLY A HANDFUL OF ROBBERS. KILLING THEM WAS EASY. BUT KILLING THE FIRE WAS A DIFFERENT MATTER.
ALL THE SAMURAI WHO HAD STILL BEEN AT THE HOUSE HAD DIED... EITHER IN FLAMES OR AT THEIR OWN HAND. SEPPUKU.
MY MASTER WAS SO ASHAMED OF HIS FAILURE TO PROTECT THE FAMILY THAT HE TOOK HIS LIFE.
SO I SHOW UP IN TIME TO SEE THE FLAMES DYING DOWN. I HAD BEEN ON A JOB IN A NEIGHBORING CITY, DELIVERING A MESSAGE.
IN HINDSIGHT, MAYBE I SHOULD'VE JOINED MY BROTHERS IN DEATH. I'D FAILED THEM, TOO.
BOTH MY MASTER AND MY MASTER'S MASTER WERE GONE, AND THE ONLY THING I CARED ABOUT WAS THIS GIRL I'D NEVER SPOKEN TO. I LOVED HER.
A BROKEN HEART DROVE ME FROM MY OLD LIFE IN THE COUNTRY.
ANOTHER BROKEN HEART IS BRINGING ME BACK.
GOOD THING MY HEART'S SO HARD. LIKE A ROCK.
A ROCK THAT'S BROKE.
SAME ROCK, DIFFERENT DAY.

SALOONS MARK THE EDGE OF THE CITY. THEY'RE THE PERFECT DOORWAY TO THE FARMLANDS.
AN IDEAL PLACE TO FIND THE INFO I NEEDED.
EXTRACTING INFORMATION IS A DELICATE PROCESS.
I'M LOOKING FOR THE BASTARD SON OF A MULE, MASTER FUYU!
ANY OF YOU SCHMUCKS HEARD OF HIM?
I'VE NEVER BEEN THE DELICATE TYPE.
WHO WANTS TO KNOW?
HIS PAPPY. SAID LIL' BOY FUYU NEEDS A SPANKIN'. I'M HERE TO DELIVER.

BINGO. AND PEOPLE SAY NAME CALLING IS POINTLESS.
WHY DO YOU DISRESPECT OUR MASTER?
I GOT BUSINESS WITH HIM AND ANYONE WHO STANDS BY HIM.
WE SHOULD KILL YOU FOR SLANDERING HIS NAME! MASTER FUYU IS A GOOD MAN!
GOOD MAN, HUH? MORE LIKE COWARDLY DOG, IF YOU ASK ME.
HOW DARE YOU CALL MASTE- GUH!

THE FOUR JOES WERE OBVIOUSLY EMPLOYED BY THIS FUYU.
THREE OF THE FOUR WERE LOW LEVEL WANNABES.
YOU CAN TELL BY HOW THEY RUN THEIR MOUTHS OFF. I RUN MY MOUTH OFF, BUT I DIDN'T DO THAT IN MY DAYS OF SERVICE.
WELL, YEAH... I GUESS I DID, BUT IT WAS ONLY WITH PEONS BELOW ME.
THE SILENT GUYS ARE ALWAYS THE TOUGHIES. IT'S A GIVEN. SHOW ME ANY ROOM AND I'LL POINT OUT THE GUY TO WATCH. THEY DON'T LOOK AT YOU, AND THEY SURE DON'T OPEN THEIR YAP.
NOT SURE WHY THEY CHOOSE NOT TO TALK. MAYBE IT MAKES THEM COOL AND MYSTERIOUS. TO ME, THEY SEEM SO CONTRIVED.
I KEPT NOSE-BLEED ALIVE. I HAD PLANS FOR HIM.
I TURNED MY ATTENTION TO MR. SILENT.

I LOVE SMACKIN' DOWN THE STRONG SILENT TYPES. I CAN KIND OF SEE WHY CHICKS DIG 'EM.
I JUST LOVE KILLIN' THEM. SO ARROGANT.
IT MUST BE THE GRACEFULNESS OF THEM. QUIET GUYS ARE ALWAYS SO DAINTY AND GRACEFUL. LIKE A LITTLE GIRL.
A LITTLE GIRL WITH A SHARP SWORD AND A HEART TO KILL.
IT WAS ANTICLIMACTIC. ALWAYS IS. YOU HOLD OUT HOPE THAT THE SILENT ONES ARE GONNA BRING THE GOODS.
AND THEN THEY LET YOU DOWN.
NOSE-BLEED! LET'S TALK.
LIKE SHOWING UP FOR SUSHI DINNER AND ALL THEY GIVE YOU IS KAPPA MAKI.
I KNOW ITS STILL SUSHI, BUT COME ON, CUCUMBER? WHERE'S THE MEAT?

YOU GOING TO TELL ME WHERE TO FIND YOUR BOSS?
ARE YOU... PLANNING TO KILL HIM?
'COURSE I WAS GOING TO KILL HIM.
LIKE I SAID. WHERE DO I FIND HIM?
I CANNOT TELL- GAH!
LEAVE HIM ALONE.
BARMAN. ARE YOU FUYU?
UM... NO.
YOU HIS BUDDY?
NO.
I'M GONNA SAY THIS REAL SLOW. YOU GET TO STAY ALIVE AS LONG AS YOU KEEP YOUR OLD MOUTH SHUT.
THIS IS BETWEEN ME AND NOSE-BLEED HERE.
TELL YOU WHAT. YOU CAN COUNT YOURSELF LUCKY. I AM GOING TO LET YOU DELIVER A MESSAGE TO YOUR BOSS.

WHAT ARE YOU DOING HERE?
WARN MASTER FUYU! THERE'S A- SCHLLG...
I THINK THAT MESSAGE WAS CLEAR ENOUGH.

I COULD SMELL THE SWEET VENGEANCE. THIS WAS THE PLACE.
I'D MAKE THEM PAY.
ALL OF THEM.

GOING OVER TO SOMEONE'S HOUSE FOR THE FIRST TIME CAN BE STRESSFUL.
DO I TAKE MY SANDALS OFF?
DO I WAIT FOR SOMEONE TO TAKE MY COAT?
DO I NEED TO BRING DRINKS? IF I DON'T, IS THAT GONNA BE AWKWARD?
IT'S PROBABLY STUPID FOR ME TO WORRY ABOUT ALL THAT, SINCE I KILLED A MAN AS SOON AS I WALKED IN THE FRONT GATE.
I THINK THEY KNEW I WASN'T THERE TO SELL THEM COOKIES.
LAY DOWN YOUR WEAPONS. MY ARCHERS ARE AT THE READY, AND YOU ARE OUTNUMBERED.
I'VE NEVER BEEN VERY GOOD WITH NUMBERS.
VERY WELL, THEN. GUARDS...

...TAKE HIM DOWN.
THE THING ABOUT ARROWS IS:
THEY'RE PRETTY FAST.
AND THEY'RE REALLY POINTY ON ONE END.
IT'S AN IMPORTANT THING TO NOTE.

BUT THERE'S A *TRICK* TO FIGHTING ARCHERS THAT THEY DON'T TEACH YA IN SCHOOL:
DON'T GET SHOT WITH AN ARROW.
EVERYTHING ELSE JUST KIND OF SORTS ITSELF OUT.

I WAS GETTING CLOSER TO FUYU. I COULD FEEL IT.
BUT UP TO THAT POINT, I'D ONLY BEEN FIGHTING WEAKLINGS... WORK-A-DAY GUARDS THAT DON'T OFFER ANY REAL PROTECTION.
THAT JUST MEANT FUYU'S BIG DOGS WERE AROUND THERE SOMEWHERE.
HALT.
BIG TALKING DOGS.
YOU TRESPASS. DIE NOW.
BIG MAN NOT SPEAK SO GOOD.
YOU CALL ME DUMB?
NO, I'M SURE YOU WERE THE TOP OF YOUR CLASS.
THAT'S WHY YOU'RE OUT HERE IN THE COLD, GUARDING ROCKS.

ME NO GUARD ROCKS! ME GUARD FUYU!
WATCHING BIG GUYS STRIKE IS LIKE WATCHING PAINT DRY.
BIG BOY MIGHT AS WELL HAVE SENT ME A LETTER EVERY TIME HE THREW A PUNCH, JUST TO LET ME KNOW.
WHEN SOMEONE FIGURES OUT HOW TO CROSS-BREED BIG, STRONG GUYS WITH SOME ACTUAL BRAINS, WE'LL BE IN A WORLD OF HURT.
BUT UNTIL THEN, FIGHTIN' THESE GUYS IS LIKE FIGHTIN' YOUR FAT GRANDMA.
DON'T ASK ME HOW I KNOW THAT.

NO MATTER HOW BIG AND BURLY THEY ARE, IF YOU STICK YOUR SWORD IN THEM, THEY'LL FALL OVER.
IT'S ONE OF THOSE NATURAL LAWS.
THE CURIOUS THING ABOUT GUYS LIKE FUYU, IS WHEN THEY HIRE GOONS, THEY HIRE THE STANDARD GOONS.
TAKE THE BIG GUY, RIGHT... PLACED AT THE FRONT FOR INTIMIDATION PURPOSES.
AFTER THAT YOU'RE BOUND TO FIND A LANKY FELLA.
PROBABLY TALL AND WITH A BIG OL' SPEAR, SWORD OR WHATEVER IS COOL WITH THE KIDS THESE DAYS.
I SEE THAT YOU HAVE BESTED MY ELDEST BROTHER IN SINGLE COMBAT.
I WILL MOURN HIM PROPERLY AFTER I HAVE DISPATCHED YOU.
HE WAS TALL ALRIGHT.
WOULD YOU LIKE A MOMENT TO REST BEFORE OUR CONFRONTATION?
I HADN'T COUNTED ON THEM HAVING A BLIND GUY THOUGH.
ANYONE WHO TRIES TO TELL YOU BLIND GUYS ARE NOTHING TO WORRY ABOUT IS A DIRTY LIAR.
YES, THANK YOU, HONORABLE SIR.
THE FACT IS, BLIND GUYS FREAK ME THE HELL OUT.

HE WAS A BRAVE WARRIOR. HIS DEMISE WILL BE MOURNED AMONG THE PEOPLE, I AM SURE.
INDEED.
MY BROTHER WAS A VALIANT MAN. WE HAVE SERVED TOGETHER SINCE YOUTH.
THIS FELLA HAD MOXY IN SPADES. TO BEAT HIM, I NEEDED TO KEEP HIM TALKING. GATHER MY WITS.
IF YOU ARE HALF THE MAN YOUR BROTHER WAS, IT WOULD BE AN HONOR TO DIE AT YOUR HANDS, IF OUR DUEL WOULD END THAT WAY.
HONORABLE BATTLE IS A RARE GEM BURIED BENEATH THE MUD OF TODAY'S MODERN WARFARE.
IT IS A BREATH OF FRESH AIR TO MEET SOMEONE WHO ADHERES TO TH- GUH!!!
LESS TALKY, MORE STABBY.

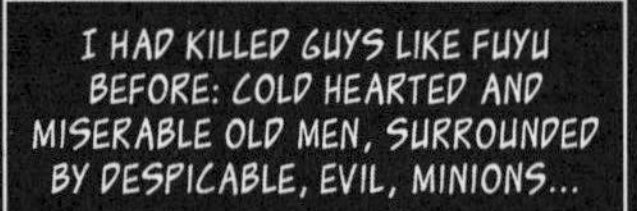
I HAD KILLED GUYS LIKE FUYU BEFORE: COLD HEARTED AND MISERABLE OLD MEN, SURROUNDED BY DESPICABLE, EVIL, MINIONS...
CONTENT TO SPEND THEIR TIME HURTING INNOCENT CHICKS LIKE JASMINE. THEY BROUGHT ALL THIS PAIN DOWN ON **THEMSELVES**, AS FAR AS I WAS CONCERNED.
FOR ALL THEIR MONEY AND POWER, THEY LACK ***IMAGINATION***.

HIGH LEVEL THUGS TEND TO COME IN ***THREES***.
BIG DUMB GUY? CHECK.

TALL FREAKY BLIND GUY? CHECK.

THAT JUST LEFT THE LITTLE, ***SNEAKY*** DUDE.

BINGO.

NEARLY INVISIBLE CLOAKED MIDGET WITH CIRCULAR THROWING BLADE?? CHECK.

PRETTY MUCH YOU JUST NEED TO WAIT THEM OUT.
IT'S LIKE HUNTING GROUNDHOGS.
IF YOU'RE PATIENT ENOUGH, THE LITTLE DEVILS EVENTUALLY STICK THEIR HEADS OUT.
THEN DOWN COMES THE SHOVEL.
I HAD TO HAND IT TO FUYU. HE LINED UP A PRETTY IMPRESSIVE CLICHE OF THUGS.
I'D EXPECTED MORE OF A FIGHT, BUT I'M NOT COMPLAINING. THEY WOULD HAVE DIED IN THE END, JUST THE SAME.
AT LEAST I STILL HAD PLENTY OF ENERGY LEFT FOR THE MASTER OF THE HOUSE.

THE TIME HAD COME TO AVENGE JASMINE'S DEATH.
IT WAS AS IF I COULD SMELL HER IN THE ROOM. I WAS REMINDED JUST THEN OF HOW MUCH MY LIFE HAD CHANGED UPON MEETING HER.
ACTUALLY, IT HADN'T REALLY CHANGED AT ALL. I LIKE TO THINK IT MIGHT'VE CHANGED.
I MIGHT HAVE BEEN A DIFFERENT MAN... SETTLED DOWN. JASMINE COULD'VE BEEN THE MOTHER OF MY FOURTEEN SAMURAI BOYS. AN ARMY OF LITTLE ME'S.
THEN WE COULD'VE ALL AVENGED JASMINE'S DEATH TOGETHER, AS A FAMILY.
FUYU!!!!!
THAT DIDN'T HAPPEN AND IT NEVER WILL. THE BEST I COULD DO THEN WAS KILL FUYU FOR ALL THE BOYS I WOULD'VE HAD. KILL HIM FOURTEEN TIMES.
MAKE IT FIFTEEN. MAYBE I WOULD'VE HAD A LITTLE GIRL SAMURAI TOO.
DEATH HAS COME TO CLAIM YOU.
DEATH HAD ARRIVED, AND WITH HIM HIS FIFTEEN ALMOST-CHILDREN.
AND WE WERE PISSED.

IN HERE, TRAVELER. IF YOU WOULDN'T MIND, PLEASE REMOVE YOUR SANDALS.
PREPARE YOURSELF, FOR VENGEANCE IS UPON YOU.
I'M SORRY. WHO ARE YOU?
SEEMED LIKE FUYU WAS GONNA PLAY COY.
AND I DON'T MEAN THE FISH.

I'M THE MAN THAT'S GOING TO MAKE YOU PAY.
IT TOOK EVERYTHING IN MY POWER NOT TO CUT HIS THROAT RIGHT THERE. BUT I WAS GOING TO OFFER HIM SOMETHING HE NEVER OFFERED JASMINE: AN HONORABLE DEATH.
I'LL LET YOU DO THE DECENT THING AND END YOUR OWN PATHETIC LIFE.
WARRIOR, WERE IT REQUIRED OF ME, I WOULD COMMIT SEPPUKU WITHOUT HESITATION.
BUT UNDER THESE CIRCUMSTANCES, I MUST STILL CONCLUDE THAT I HAVE NO IDEA WHO YOU ARE.
OLD MAN WAS SLICK, BUT I WASN'T ABOUT TO LET HIM WEASEL HIS WAY OUT THAT EASILY.
YOU KILLED MY GIRL.

LET ME SEE THAT.
THERE IT WAS... THE CRACK IN THE LEVEE.
I'VE SEEN IT A THOUSAND TIMES. CONFRONT A MAN WITH UNMISTAKABLE EVIDENCE OF HIS CRIMES AND HE CRUMBLES LIKE ROTTEN WOOD.
WHERE DID YOU GET THIS?
A BROKEN LEVEE CAN ONLY HOLD BACK THE RIVER FOR SO LONG.
HER NAME WAS JASMINE. SHE WAS HOLDING IT WHEN SHE DIED. IT'S ALL I HAVE LEFT.
OH... OH GOD.
USUALLY THAT WHOLE LEVEE METAPHOR ISN'T QUITE SO LITERAL.

SHE... SHE...
SHE WAS MY NIECE.
YOU KILLED YOUR OWN NIECE?
NO, YOU IDIOT! I HAD NOTHING TO DO WITH HER DEATH.
WHEN THE HITMEN FELL, THEY FINGERED YOU AS THE BOSSMAN.
AND YOU'RE GULLIBLE ENOUGH TO BELIEVE WHAT EVERY TWO-BIT CRIMINAL TELLS YOU?
I SUPPOSE I MAY AS WELL EXPLAIN IT TO YOU. MY PAST, IT SEEMS, HAS CAUGHT UP WITH ME.

IT SEEMS A DIFFERENT LIFE... A DISTANT REALITY, WHERE I WAS A DIFFERENT MAN. TEN YEARS AGO, YOUR ASSESSMENT OF ME WOULD HAVE BEEN ACCURATE.
I LORDED OVER THE CITY WITH MY DEAREST FRIEND, NATSU. WE HAD ANY NUMBER OF COMPANIONS, AN OVERABUNDANCE OF RESOURCES, AND THE POWER TO CONTROL ANYONE WE WISHED.
OUR ENEMIES TREMBLED BEFORE US, AND WE RULED THE CITY WITH IRON FISTS. WITH A WORD SPOKEN, GROWN MEN SHUDDERED...
...AND FELL.

A VOID GREW DEEP WITHIN. A THIRST UNQUENCHABLE WITH THE MYRIAD OF THINGS I FED IT. NEARLY CONSUMED, I SOUGHT ISOLATION AND YEARNED FOR FREEDOM.
YOU MUST UNDERSTAND, A MAN IN MY POSITION WAS MORE A PRISONER THAN ANY SERVANT, OR SOLDIER.
I HAD TO ESCAPE THAT LIFE, NO MATTER THE COST.
I BENT THE EAR OF MY ONLY AND DEAREST FRIEND, NATSU. HE COULD HAVE KILLED ME. HE SHOULD HAVE KILLED ME. INSTEAD, HE OFFERED ME A WAY OUT.
I TOOK IT.

NOT EVERYONE WAS HAPPY ABOUT MY DEPARTURE. LEAST OF WHICH WAS NATSU'S ELDEST DAUGHTER, **AKINA**.
SUFFICE IT TO SAY, I THINK SHE WOULD HAVE SLIT MY THROAT WHEN I LEFT, HAD SHE BEEN GIVEN THE CHANCE.
INSTEAD, SHE JUST WATCHED ME WALK OUT OF THAT WORLD FOREVER, **ABANDONING** IT.
ABANDONING **HER**.

SO LET ME GET THIS STRAIGHT... YOU'RE TELLING ME SOME DAME YOU CROSSED TEN YEARS AGO SUDDENLY WENT AND FRAMED YOU FOR KILLING THE GIRL I LOVED?
WHY DID IT TAKE SO LONG?
PATIENCE, SAMURAI. I HAVEN'T FINISHED MY STORY YET.
MAY I OFFER YOU SOME TEA?
SOUNDS GOOD.
IT WAS GOOD TEA.

AS I WAS SAYING, I EMBRACED MY NEW LIFE. WHEN I ARRIVED HERE, THIS WAS A POOR, RURAL COMMUNITY OF UNEMPLOYED FARMERS AND LABORERS.
I PROVIDED WORK FOR MANY GOOD MEN... TRAINING THEM IN THE WAYS OF HONOR AND VIRTUE. WITH THEM, I REBUILT THIS VILLAGE INTO THE NOBLE PLACE IT IS TODAY.
BUT FOR ALL MY ATTEMPTS TO ATONE FOR MY PAST TRANSGRESSIONS, THE PAST HAS A WAY OF CATCHING UP WITH PEOPLE.
YOU SEE, MY OLD FRIEND NATSU PASSED AWAY RECENTLY.

WITH HER FATHER GONE, AKINA INHERITED ALL THAT WAS ONCE HIS. INCLUDING ALL OF HIS DEBTS AND PROMISES.

AKINA'S DISDAIN FOR ME WAS NO SECRET, BUT FOR HER TO DEAL WITH ME AS SHE WOULD LIKE TO WOULD HAVE BEEN A VIOLATION OF ALL HER FATHER HAD SET IN PLACE.

IT WOULD SEEM THAT MY NIECE'S DEATH WAS ONLY THE FIRST OF MANY IN HER BIZARRE SCHEME OF REVENGE, AND THAT YOUR BLIND RAGE WAS THE THREAD THAT WOVE IT ALL TOGETHER.
I WILL TAKE IT UPON MYSELF TO AVENGE JASMINE'S DEATH FOR BOTH OF US.
SO YOU'RE JUST GOING TO TAKE MY WORD FOR ALL THAT?
HOW DO YOU KNOW I'M NOT LYING AS WELL?
IT'S REAL SIMPLE: IF YOU'RE LYING, I'LL COME BACK AND KILL YOU. IF YOU'RE NOT, I OWE YOU ONE FOR SLAYING ALL YOUR MEN.
SORRY ABOUT THAT, BY THE WAY.
BOY, WAS MY FACE RED. AND I DON'T JUST MEAN FROM ALL THE BLOOD.

I WOULDN'T CONSIDER MY TRIP TO THE COUNTRYSIDE TO BE A *TOTAL* WASTE.

AT LEAST I HAD A CLEARER PICTURE OF WHO WAS TO BLAME FOR OFFING JASMINE.

I'D TEACH THIS AKINA WHAT YOU GET FOR TREATING SAM NOIR LIKE A *PAWN*.

SAM AIN'T *NOBODY'S* PAWN. HE'S A *KNIGHT*. A KNIGHT WITH TWO *SWORDS*.

AND EVERYONE KNOWS KNIGHTS COME AT YOU ALL *CRAZY*-LIKE. ONE-UP, TWO-OVER... TWO-BACKWARDS, ONE-TO-THE-SIDE... YOU NEVER *KNOW*.

I'D DRAG AKINA UP AND DOWN THIS WHOLE CHESSBOARD.

TO BE CONTINUED...

IT FELT GOOD TO BE BACK IN THE BIG CITY.
THE CLEAN AIR.
THERE WAS A NEW SCENT THAT NIGHT THOUGH.
THE SWEET SMELL OF REVENGE.
AKINA PROBABLY THOUGHT I'D LONG SINCE KILLED FUYU. THAT I'D DONE HER DIRTY WORK FOR HER.
SHE WAS PROBABLY LAUGHING ALL THE WAY TO THE BANK.
HOW ME KILLING FUYU WOULD'VE MADE HER ANY MONEY IS BESIDE THE POINT.
SHE WAS LAUGHING. I COULD FEEL IT.

AKINA HAD SOME SWEET DIGS.
A REAL REPUTABLE LOOKING BASE OF OPERATIONS.
LOTS OF JOES IN STARCHED SUITS AND SNAPPY TIES.
GOOD EVENING SIR.
I FELT LIKE A BULL IN A FINE CHINA STORE.
MAY I WELCOME YOU TO THE OFFICES OF-
GAHH!
ONLY UNLIKE THE BULL, I WASN'T THERE TO SHOP.

HEY, FELLA. YOU JUST MADE YOURSELF A HUGE MISTAKE.
YOU GOT ANY IDEA WHERE YOU ARE?
ISN'T THIS THE TERIYAKI HOUSE?
I WOULD HAVE ASSUMED SO FROM ALL THE LIMP NOODLES I SEE LAYIN' AROUND HERE.
THOSE PENGUIN SUITS MADE THEM LOOK LIKE CERTIFIED ACCOUNTANTS.
I'LL BRING AKINA YOUR HEAD ON A PLATE!
WHY DO WISEGUYS ALWAYS THINK THEY'RE SO TOUGH?
WHAT WAS HE GONNA DO, BEAT ME WITH HIS ABACUS?

WHO CAME UP WITH THE ABACUS IN THE FIRST PLACE?
PUSHIN' THOSE LITTLE COLORED BEADS AROUND ON STICKS? IT'S LIKE A BUSY-BOX FOR ADULTS.
WHY CAN'T THOSE GUYS ADD NUMBERS ON THEIR FINGERS LIKE EVERYONE ELSE?
MATH IS FOR SUCKERS. REAL MEN COUNT WITH THEIR FISTS.
ANYWAY, WHERE WAS I?
OH, RIGHT.

SO THEN THE RECEPTIONIST TRIPPED THE ALARM.
GUAAAAAARDS! INTRUDER!!!!! GUAAAAAARDS!! ALAAAARM!!
YOU'D THINK AKINA COULD HAVE AT LEAST HIRED A HOT SECRETARY.
BUT THIS WHALE, SHE WAS WAILIN'. REALLY GETTIN' ON MY NERVES.
ALARM! ALARM! ALARM! ALARM! ALARM! ALARM! ALARM!
WHOA, WHOA... SETTLE DOWN THERE, SALLY. THIS ISN'T WHAT IT LOOKS LIKE...
GUARDS! ALAAARM!!!!
GENERALLY, DAMES ARE MY SOFT SPOT.
EAAASY THERE BESSIE. SHHHH. IT'S ALL RIGHT...
AS IT TURNS OUT, SOFT SPOTS ARE A GREAT PLACE TO STICK A SWORD.

SO MUCH FOR THE ELEMENT OF SURPRISE.
I WAS ON AKINA'S HOME TURF NOW, AND I NEEDED TO STAY ON MY TOES.
THE WELCOMING COMMITTEE WENT DOWN EASY, BUT I KNEW THERE WERE PLENTY MORE GOONS NEARBY.
AND THE NEXT WAVE WAS LIKELY TO BE A LITTLE LESS CORDIAL AND A LITTLE MORE DEADLY.
NO PROBLEM. I CAN DEAL WITH DEADLY.
I BUTTER MY TOAST WITH DEADLY.

HEY WALLY, HEY JANET. SORRY I'M LATE FOR MY SHIFT...
HAD TO FIX A BURST PIPE UP ON... UH...
HI.
I... I... YOU...
HI.
HERE'S HOW THIS IS GONNA WORK. YOU TELL ME WHERE AKINA IS, OR I START BREAKING EVERY BONE IN YOUR HAND.
ELEVATOR. TOP FLOOR. I JUST WORK HERE, MAC.
THANKS BUDDY. SORRY ABOUT THE MESS.

FORM UP, MEN! I WANT ARCHERS IN POSITION! SCATTERED FORMATION!
I'LL HAND IT TO AKINA. HER PEOPLE WERE ORGANIZED.
NATSU HAD TRAINED THEM WELL.
IN A WAY, THOSE MEN WERE BEING USED JUST AS MUCH AS I HAD BEEN.
I'M SURE AKINA HAD THEM ALL THINKING THEY WERE ABOUT TO FACE THE MAN WHO KILLED THEIR BELOVED NATSU.
SHE HAD PROBABLY TOLD THEM I WAS SOME KIND OF DEMON.
SOME KIND OF MONSTER.
STEADY, MEN! HOLD FAST AND WAIT FOR MY SIGNAL!

BUT I AIN'T NO DEMON MONSTER.
I'M JUST A MAN.
FIRE!!!
AND SOMETIMES, MEN MAKE MISTAKES.

THIS TIME, THE MISTAKE WAS THEIRS.
IT'S NOT HIM!
STAY ALERT MEN, WE'VE GOT US A RAT.
USUALLY, I DON'T LIKE TO GO THE WHOLE SNEAKY-SNEAKY ROUTE...
BUT A MAN'S GOTTA HAVE PRIORITIES, AND IN THIS CASE IT WAS TIME FOR ME TO GET MY REVENGE ON.
HE'S HERE! HE'S HERE!

REVENGE ALWAYS GETS A BAD RAP.
LIKE PEOPLE ARE ASHAMED OF IT OR SOMETHING.
THEY'RE ALWAYS SENDIN' BIRTHDAY CARDS AND ANNIVERSARY CARDS...
BUT NO ONE EVER SENDS AN "I'M GONNA KILL YOU" CARD.
I THINK THOSE THINGS WOULD SELL LIKE HOTCAKES. I'D BUY 'EM.
HELL, I SHOULD MAKE MY OWN.
THAT'S A GOOD IDEA.
"GREETINGS FROM SAM. YOU'RE A DEAD MAN, SUKKA."
BIG OL' PICTURE OF ME ON THE FRONT. WHO WOULDN'T WANT ONE OF THOSE?

NOW, DON'T GET ME WRONG.
I DON'T CONDONE MINDLESS KILLING.
BUT AS FAR AS I WAS CONCERNED, THESE MEN WERE *ALREADY* DEAD.

THEY WERE JUST A FLOOD OF CORPSES I HAD TO PADDLE THROUGH ON MY WAY UP THE RIVER.
AND AT THE END OF THAT RIVER, I WOULD FIND AKINA.

LOOKS LIKE JUST YOU AND ME LEFT, BUB.
NOT TO WORRY, RONIN. MORE SOLDIERS WILL BE HERE SOON.
AND IN THE MEANTIME, WE CAN DUEL LIKE MEN. AS SAMURAI.
YOU SEEM LIKE A STAND-UP FELLA.
WHAT ARE YOU DOING WORKING FOR A DISHONORABLE SCUM SUCKER LIKE AKINA?
THE PAY IS GOOD AND THE WORK IS STEADY.
WHO ARE YOU TO TALK? YOU JUST KILLED TWO DOZEN MEN.
YES, BUT I DID IT OUT OF LOVE.
NOW, ARE WE GOING TO FIGHT, OR ARE YOU GOING TO STEP ASIDE AND LET ME TAKE CARE OF MY BUSINESS?
I WILL STAND MY GROUND. I DO NOT FEAR YOU.
HAVE IT YOUR WAY.

THERE ARE A LOT OF MISCONCEPTIONS ABOUT WHAT IT'S LIKE WHEN TWO TRAINED SAMURAI DUEL.
THE MYTH IS THAT THERE'S ALL KINDS OF PARRYING AND LUNGING AND FANCY FOOTWORK.
BUT REALLY, IT'S A LOT MORE LIKE TWO SHIPS PASSING IN THE NIGHT. ONLY FASTER.
AND THEN ONE OF THOSE SHIPS DIES.

I HAD REACHED MY DESTINATION.
ALL THAT STOOD BETWEEN ME AND THE FINISH LINE WAS A WOODEN DOOR AND ONE SWING OF MY BLADE.
I LOCKED UP BEHIND MYSELF...
WANTED A LITTLE PRIVACY.
YOU MUST BE AKINA.
AND YOU MUST BE SAM NOIR. I HAVE TO CONFESS, I NEVER THOUGHT WE'D ACTUALLY MEET.
WORD IS THAT YOU'VE BEEN QUITE A BUSY BOY.
YOUR TRICK DIDN'T WORK.
IF YOU WANTED FUYU DEAD, YOU SHOULD HAVE KILLED HIM YOURSELF... IT'S NO BUSINESS OF MINE.
YOUR BIG MISTAKE WAS PULLING JASMINE INTO ALL THIS. WITH THAT, YOU SIGNED YOUR DEATH WARRANT.

JASMINE WAS NOTHING BUT BAIT TO BEGIN WITH. JUST A WORM ON A HOOK.
AND ABOUT AS VALUABLE AS ONE, TOO.
YOU SHUT YOUR DIRTY MOUTH. JASMINE WAS INNOCENT.
YOU TURNED OUT TO BE SMARTER THAN I THOUGHT. A SHAME, REALLY.
BUT AT LEAST NOW YOU CAN JOIN YOUR HUSSY IN DEATH!
AKINA'S CRUEL WORDS SHOT THROUGH ME LIKE A KNIFE.
HRRRGHH...
OR MAYBE IT WAS THE ACTUAL KNIFE, I'M NOT REALLY SURE.

WHATEVER WAS CAUSING IT, THE PAIN FUELED ME.
IT STOKED THE FURNACE OF RAGE DEEP INSIDE ME LIKE A BELLOWS.
THE EMBERS OF MY LOVE FOR JASMINE GLOWED RED AND THEN BURST INTO FLAME.
IT WAS MUCH TOO LATE FOR AKINA OR ANY OF HER HENCHMEN TO PUT THAT FIRE OUT.
EXCEPT, OF COURSE, BY QUENCHING IT WITH AKINA'S TRAITOROUS BLOOD.
THIS ENDS HERE.

YOU HAVE ANYTHING TO SAY FOR YOURSELF BEFORE I FINISH YOUR MISERABLE LIFE?
YES.
KILLING ME SOLVES NOTHING.
THIS BUILDING IS FILLED WITH HUNDREDS OF MY LOYAL FIGHTERS. THEY WILL DESTROY YOU.
YOUR FATE IS SEALED.
AND KILLING ME WON'T BRING YOUR PRECIOUS JASMINE BACK. KILLING ME WON'T-
SORRY TO CUT YOU OFF THERE.
I WAS KINDA HOPING YOU DIDN'T HAVE ANYTHING TO SAY.

AND THAT'S WHEN I SAW YOU.
MY FIRST THOUGHT WAS: "AWWW, CRAP. I HOPE I DIDN'T JUST KILL THAT LITTLE KID'S MOM IN FRONT OF HIM."
I MEAN, I STILL WOULD HAVE, SEEING AS HOW SHE WAS EVIL AND ALL.
BUT COLOR ME RELIEVED TO FIND OUT THAT YOU'RE JUST THE SERVANT BOY.
SO WHAT DO YA SAY, KID...
YOU EVER THOUGHT OF BECOMING A DETECTIVE?
NO SIR, MY ELDERS HAVE SERVED THIS FAMILY FOR SIX GENERATIONS.
I AM THE YOUNGEST APPRENTICE, AND SOMEDAY WHEN I AM OLDER, I WILL BE-
THAT'S GOOD KID. REAL GOOD. YOU DON'T WANT THIS LIFE ANYWAY.
IT'S FULL OF HEARTACHE AND REGRET.
THE THINGS YOU LOVE GET TAKEN AWAY AND YOU'RE LEFT WITH A HANDFUL OF REVENGE.
THEY SAY REVENGE LEAVES A MAN EMPTY INSIDE.
I SAY THAT JUST LEAVES MORE ROOM FOR SUSHI AND BEER.

MORE WATER, SIR?
GLADLY.
THANKS FOR THE PIT STOP, KID. THAT REALLY HIT THE SPOT.
YOU MIGHT WANNA GO HIDE SOMEWHERE NOW.
I GOT MORE UGLY BUSINESS TO ATTEND TO.

ALL RIGHT FELLAS, WHO'S NEXT?
NOBODY PLAYS SAM NOIR.
NOBODY.
THE END.

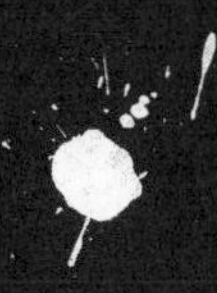

Chapter Two

RONIN HOLIDAY

I *FAILED* HER.
I LEFT HER THERE ON MY OFFICE FLOOR AND RAN OFF INTO THE NIGHT LIKE A CRAZED ANIMAL.
SURE, I TOLD MYSELF IT WAS ALL ABOUT AVENGING HER DEATH, BUT WHAT WAS IT *REALLY*?
WAS IT ABOUT ME RUNNING FROM MY OWN SHAME?
HIDING MY GUILT UNDER A PILE OF BODIES?
IN MY LINE OF WORK, FAILURE DOESN'T GO DOWN EASY.
IT'S A BITTER PILL THAT GETS STUCK IN YOUR THROAT AND WON'T GO AWAY NO MATTER HOW MUCH WATER YOU DRINK.
EVEN THE *WHISKEY* WON'T DISSOLVE IT AWAY.
MY MASTER SHOWED ME QUITE CLEARLY WHAT THE PRICE OF *FAILURE* WAS.
THE PRICE OF *SHAME*.
I HAD FAILED JASMINE, AND I HAD FAILED MYSELF.
IT WAS TIME FOR ME TO STAND UP AND BE A *MAN*. TO DO THE THING I SHOULD HAVE DONE LONG AGO.
IT WAS TIME FOR ME TO GO TO A BETTER PLACE.

SO I WENT TO THE BEACH.
NOT JUST ANY BEACH THOUGH...
I WENT WHERE THE SAND IS WHITE AND THE WATER'S BLUE AND WATCHING PASSERS-BY IS LIKE BEING AT A BUFFET.
YOU GOT YOUR DAMES, BROADS AND BETTIES ALL UNDER ONE HEAT LAMP.
SURE, THERE ARE SOME FAT JOES THERE TOO, BUT THEY'RE LIKE THE GREASY WONTON NO ONE PUTS ON THEIR PLATE.

AFTER A HEAPING PORTION OF CHICKS AND A SIDE OF FINE LADIES, I'D BE STUFFED ALL WEEK.

I DON'T GET TO GO ON VACATION VERY OFTEN, WHAT WITH MY HIGH PROFILE CAREER AND ALL.
BUT WHEN I DO, I LIKE TO MEET UP WITH MY THREE GOOD FRIENDS AS OFTEN AS POSSIBLE.
MISTER COLADA.
DOCTOR TAI.
AND THE EVER SO TASTY MISS TINI.
I CALL HER MISS 'CAUSE SHE'S SLENDER IN THE MIDDLE, LIKE THE BELLE OF THE BALL.
ME AND MY BUDDIES, WE GO EVERYWHERE TOGETHER.
SOMETIMES I TAKE 'EM OUT TO SHOWS, TO LET THEM KNOW HOW MUCH I CARE.
AND THEY AIN'T NO CHEAP DATE, EITHER.. ESPECIALLY AFTER THE FOURTH OR FIFTH ROUND.
BUT MY GIRL TINI, SHE KNOWS HOW TO TREAT A MAN RIGHT.

GETTIN' OUT OF THE BIG CITY MEANS LEAVING ALL MY TROUBLES BEHIND.
I GET TO SET ASIDE THE SAMURAI DETECTIVE FOR A BIT AND JUST BE ME: SAM NOIR.
IT'S RARE TO GET A LITTLE ME TIME.
I EAT IT UP EVERY CHANCE I GET.
AND LIKE CLOCKWORK, WITHOUT FAIL, SOME SCHMUCK TRIES TO WHACK ME WHEN MY GUARD IS DOWN.
IT'S ALMOST BECOME A LITTLE GAME FOR ME.
SEEING HOW LONG I CAN GO BEFORE SOMEONE COMES A GUNNING.
SO FAR, MY RECORD IS EIGHTEEN HOURS.
THIS TRIP, I DIDN'T EVEN MAKE IT TWELVE.

USUALLY, IT'S JUST YOUR TYPICAL BARFIGHT.
OR MAYBE THE MEATHEAD BOYFRIEND WHO DIDN'T MUCH LIKE THE WAY I WAS TALKING TO HIS LADY.
BUT THIS WAS DIFFERENT.
THIS GUY WAS NO LOCAL...
HE LOOKED MORE LIKE HE WAS FROM MY NECK O' THE WOODS.
THAT ONLY MEANT I KNEW EXACTLY HOW TO TALK TO HIM.

IT'S CUZ SOME OTHER GUY JUMPED ON MY BACK AND WRAPPED A PIANO WIRE AROUND MY NECK.

IN EITHER CASE, MY TUNE WAS ABOUT UP.

I NEVER DID LIKE THE PIANO MUCH.

I'M MORE OF A SAXOPHONE MAN.

THIS NEXT PART'S A BIT HAZY, BUT FROM WHAT I REMEMBER, THAT'S WHEN THE FELLA WITH THE BIRD SHOWED UP.
I DIDN'T ASK FOR NO HELP, BUT I WASN'T ABOUT TO LOOK A GIFT HORSE IN THE MOUTH.
ACTUALLY, I DID THAT ONCE.
I WOULDN'T RECOMMEND IT.
STUPID THING THOUGHT MY NOSE WAS A CARROT.

ONE SIDE, STRANGER.
THIS ONE'S STILL SUCKIN' AIR.
I WAS LUCKY TO STILL BE SUCKIN' AIR.
CAN I HELP YOU UP, FRIEND?
SCREW OFF, YOU MISSED ONE.
AYE, THERE'S THREE.
HE WON'T GET FAR.

SORRY TO LEAVE YOU HANGING OVER THE DECK THERE, BUT I HAD TO WAIT FOR THEM TO MAKE THEIR MOVE.
AND WHO THE HELL ARE *YOU* EXACTLY?
EDMUND C. GROG, ISLAND DETECTIVE.
THAT'S A FANCY TITLE THERE, EDDIE. ***I*** GOT ME ONE OF THEM, TOO.
NOW IF YOU'LL EXCUSE ME, I'M GONNA HEAD BACK TO MY ROOM, GET MY STUFF, AND FIND OUT WHO'S GOT IT OUT FOR ME ***THIS*** TIME.

YOU LOST, BOY?
WHY ARE YOU FOLLOWING ME AROUND LIKE A LONELY PUPPY?
RUN OFF AND FIND YOUR MASTER.
YOU TOOK QUITE A BEATING BACK THERE...
FIGURED YOU MIGHT NEED A BODYGUARD TO WATCH YOUR BACK.
YOU BEST WATCH YOUR MOUTH, SON - OR YOU'RE LIABLE TO GET IT CUT OFF. YOU EVEN KNOW WHO YOU'RE TALKIN' TO?
AYE. YOU'RE SAM NOIR.
BEEN WATCHIN' YOU SINCE YOU GOT HERE, TOO.
SORRY TO RUIN YOUR SCHOOLGIRL CRUSH, BUT I AIN'T NO QUARTERBACK AND YOU SURE AS HELL AIN'T NO CHEERLEADER.
NOW GET OUT OF MY ROOM. I'VE GOT WORK TO DO.

YOU'RE NOT THE ONLY DETECTIVE ON THIS ISLAND, MR. NOIR. I'VE BEEN ON THIS CASE FOR WEEKS.
I'M NOT LETTING YOU OUT OF MY SIGHT UNTIL I FIND OUT WHO IS BEHIND THIS.
LISTEN PAL, I SAVED YOUR BARNACLED ASS BACK THERE.
WELL, FINDING OUT WHO'S BEHIND THIS IS MY JOB NOW. WHY'RE YOU SO HOT ON THIS CASE? WHO HIRED YOU, ANYWAY?
HIRED ME? SAM, I'M A POLICE DETECTIVE. THIS ENTIRE ISLAND IS MY JURISDICTION.
POLICE? DAMN, AND HERE I THOUGHT YOU WERE A RESPECTABLE PRIVATE DICK.
TURNS OUT YOU'RE JUST A DICK.
SAM NOIR DON'T NEED SAVIN'.
NOW I'M GONNA GET MY COAT AND YOU'RE GONNA GET THE HELL OUT OF MY WAY.

CA-
RAAAAWWK!
AND TAKE THAT PARAKEET WITH YOU, BEFORE HE CRAPS ON THE RUG.
BE QUIET, WATSON'S TALKING.
RAAAAWWK!
I NEVER DID GET USED TO EDDIE CHATTIN' WITH HIS BIRD LIKE THAT.
IT AIN'T NATURAL.
I THINK WATSON MAY HAVE JUST FOUND OUR THIRD SUSPECT.
UUUUGGH...

SMART BIRD.
TIME TO SING, CHUMP. WHO'S AFTER ME THIS TIME?
IS IT THE TRIAD?
YAKUZA LOU?
IS IT TANAKA'S CREW FROM DAGGER GANG?
JACKY THE NOOSE?
WHO HIRED YOU, DAMMIT?
THE MAN WHO HIRED ME. HE GOES BY THE NAME... UGGRRHH
EDDIE, ARE YOU INSANE?!?
QUITE THE OPPOSITE. I'M JUST SAVING US SOME TROUBLE.

HOW ARE WE SUPPOSED TO FIND OUT WHO SENT HIM IF HE CAN'T TELL US!?!
WHAT KIND OF AMATEUR COP ARE YOU?
RULE NUMBER ONE: CRIMINALS LIE. IF HE HAD TOLD US A NAME, CHANCES ARE IT WOULD JUST BE MISDIRECTION.
I CAN'T REALLY SAY I DISAGREED WITH THE MAN.
TRUSTING THE WORD OF THUGS HAS LED ME DOWN THE WRONG PATH BEFORE.
POOR OLD FUYU.
SO WHAT'S YOUR PLAN THEN, SMART GUY?
PILLAGE THE CORPSE FOR CLUES, AND LET THE EVIDENCE LEAD US.
THERE 'TIS. A HARBOR TOKEN. AND I THINK I KNOW JUST WHERE TO START.

WITH MY ONLY SUSPECT DEAD, I FIGURED I'D LET EDDIE PLAY COPS N' ROBBERS FOR A WHILE.
WE ENDED UP DOWN AT THE PIER.
HEY OLD MAN. YOU MIND IF WE ASK YOU SOME QUESTIONS?
NAY, 'TIS FINE, MATEY. TOW YER ROPE.
WE'RE LOOKING FOR THE SHIP THAT MIGHT'VE GIVEN OUT THIS BOARDING TOKEN TO ONE OF ITS PASSENGERS.
CAN YOU LEND US A HAND?
AYE, ME BUCKO. THOUGH YE DONE BLOWN IN ON A STRANGE WIND. BEFORE I SPIN YOU A FINE YARN, WHAT SAY YE FETCH ME A BOTTLE O' GINGER RUM OR A LADY OF EXPANSIVE SENSIBILITIES.
MAYBE A LI'L O' EACH.
I AIN'T HERE TO BARTER, POPS. YOU CAN START SPILLIN' INFORMATION OR YOUR GUTS.
YOUR CHOICE.
YE DON'T SHIVER ME, YE WAISTER. THIS OLD EYE O' MINE SEEN SIGHTS THAT'D MAKE YE CURL BACK UP INTO YER MAMA'S GUT.
NOW IF IT'S QUERIES YE WANT ANSWERED, MAYHAPS I CAN DREDGE ME THOUGHTS FOR A BIT O' SHINY.
LET ME HANDLE THIS.

THIS SHINY ENOUGH FOR YOU, PEGGY?
AYE, AYE. THAT'LL DO, SEA DOG.
'TWAS FOUR DAYS PAST AND A RED TIDE. THE MEN YE BE SEEKIN' UNLOADED THEIR DUFFELS FROM A SLOOP ON THIS VERY PIER.
USED TO SAIL WITH ITS CAPTAIN, MESELF. BLAGGARD CHEATED ME OUTTA' ME FAIR SHARE OF A HAUL, AND I DON'T MUCH MIND RATTIN' HIM OUT.
SHIP BY THE NAME OF THE FLYIN' POPE. YE NEED A LINE TO HANG HIM WITH?
WE'RE NOT HERE TO KILL HIM, PEGGY. JUST NEED A BIT OF INFO.
CATCH YOU AROUND, DOLLFACE. YOU MIGHT WANNA GET THAT LEG LOOKED AT.

I THINK WE FOUND OUR BOAT.
SWABBY! COME ON DOWN HERE FOR A MINUTE. WE'VE GOT SOME QUESTIONS FOR YA.
WHO'RE YOU?
ISLAND POLICE, KID. GET A MOVE ON.
MAKE ME, FLATFOOT! YOU'LL NEVER TAKE ME ALIVE!
STUPID PIRATE KIDS. THEY NEVER LEARN.
I'LL BE RIGHT BACK.

AHH, REBELLIOUS YOUTH.
REMINDS ME OF ME.
AND IF THERE'S ONE THING YOUNG PUNKS LIKE THAT NEED, IT'S SOME COLD HARD DISCIPLINE.
OR A COLD FISH TO THE BACK OF THE HEAD, IF THAT'S ALL YOU HAVE HANDY.
YOU GOT SPUNK, KID, BUT YOU PICKED THE WRONG JOE TO RUN ON.
I'M NOT AFRAID OF YOU, COPPER.
I'M NO COP, AND YOU DON'T KNOW THE MEANING OF AFRAID.

SING FOR ME, KID. THREE MEN HIRED PASSAGE ON THIS BOAT FOUR DAYS AGO. WHO WERE THEY?
I DON'T KNOW, I SWEARS! I ONLY CARRIED THEIR STUFF...
I'M JUST A DECKHAND!
CARRIED THEIR STUFF WHERE?
I... UHH... A MILE UPRIVER. THE ABANDONED MILL.
I SWEARS, I SWEARS!
YOU GOT AN INTERESTING TECHNIQUE THERE, SAM.
I GOT ANSWERS, DIDN'T I? YOU KNOW OF THAT OLD MILL?
I SURE DO.
YOU GONNA LEAD THE WAY, OR YOU JUST WANNA STAND HERE AND HOLD HANDS?

I HAVEN'T BEEN OUT HERE IN QUITE SOME TIME.
PLACE SURE HAS GONE TO *CRAP*.
HOODLUMS GOTTA HAVE A HIDEOUT. IF WE'RE *LUCKY*, WHOEVER HIRED THEM IS HANGING OUT HERE TOO.
I THINK WE SHOULD SCOUT AROUND A LITTLE BIT FIRST. GET THE LAY OF THE LAND.
YOU HAVE FUN WITH THAT. I'M GONNA DO THIS LIKE WE DO IT BACK IN THE *CITY*...
CATCH 'EM WITH THEIR *PANTS* DOWN.

WELCOME, SAM NOIR...
WELCOME TO YOUR DEATH!
I HAD A DREAM JUST LIKE THAT, ONCE.
ONLY THE RHINO WAS WEARIN' A TOP HAT.
TO BE CONTINUED...

NORMALLY, I'M NOT A GUY THAT'S VERY EASY TO SURPRISE. BUT I GOTTA HAND IT TO THE CRAZY JUNGLE LADY.
PET KILLER RHINO?
YEAH, THAT GOT MY ATTENTION.

SAM!
I COULD TELL EDDIE WAS MORE THAN A BIT SURPRISED.
LIKE A LITTLE KID ON CHRISTMAS MORNING WHO GETS A COBRA INSTEAD OF A TRAIN SET.
YOU KNOW - THE JUMPY TYPE.
GIVE UP NOW, SAM. YOU'RE DEAD ALREADY.
I'M DEAD WHEN I SAY I'M DEAD, GIRLY.
CHICK WAS HOT, BUT A LITTLE BOSSY. TOO BAD.
I MIGHT'VE ASKED HER OUT.

EDDIE SEEMED TO THINK SHE WAS A LOOKER TOO, BECAUSE HE WAS TRYING TO MAKE A MOVE.
MUST HAVE LOWER STANDARDS THAN ME.
CALL OFF YOUR RHINO IF YOU WANT TO LIVE.
I'LL CALL HIM OFF ONCE I HAVE BOTH OF YOUR HEADS!
I FELT BAD FOR EDDIE. SHE WAS PLAYIN' HARD TO GET.

I ONLY GET PAID FOR SAM, BUT IT'S YOUR LUCKY DAY.
I'LL KILL YOU FOR FREE.
AHH, SO YOU'RE JUST A HIRED THUG TOO, THEN.
I FIGURED YOU WERE SOMEONE MORE IMPORTANT, WHAT WITH THE THEATRICS AND ALL.
HOW DARE YOU?!?
I'M MORE WARRIOR THAN YOU COULD EVER DREAM TO BE IN A THOUSAND LIFETIMES!

THEY SHOULD HAVE RHINO *RODEOS*.

ONE TIME I WENT TO A *REGULAR* RODEO, AND ALL THEY RODE WERE *BULLS*. I CALL THAT A WASTE OF MY TIME.

NOW YOU PUT A COUPLE COWBOYS ON THE BACK OF A STAMPEDING *RHINO* AND YOU'VE GOT YOURSELF A SHOW.

AND THOSE *RODEO CLOWNS* - IF THEY GOT IN THE WRONG PLACE AT THE WRONG TIME - THEY'D POP LIKE A WATER BALLOON AT A PORCUPINE PARTY.

YOU CALL YOURSELF A WARRIOR, BUT YOU LACK DISCIPLINE. IT REMINDS ME OF THE SWABBIES WE USED TO KEEL HAUL JUST FOR STEPPING OUT OF LINE.
A WORD OF ADVICE: I'D LOSE THE TEMPER, IF I WERE YOU.
OOOOF.
YOU RODENT! YOU INSOLENT PIG!
I'D HAVE TO HANDLE THE BIG FELLA MYSELF. NO DIFFERENT THAN WHAT I'M USED TO.
EDDIE WAS STILL TOO BUSY MACKIN' ON HIS DATE TO BE ANY HELP.
C'MERE FLUFFY. COME GIVE SAM A BIG HUG.

LISTEN UP, ED. WE GOT AN INCOMING RHINO ON YOUR SIX.
WHEN I GIVE THE SIGNAL, YOU HIT THE DIRT.
AYE. WHAT'S THE SIGNAL?
THIS.
AAAAAHH!
AHHH, TEAMWORK. I LOVE IT WHEN A PLAN COMES TOGETHER.

ONE RHINO, ON THE ROCKS.
DAMN, THAT SOUNDS LIKE A MIGHTY FINE DRINK.
I BET IT'S GOT *PINEAPPLE* IN IT.
WHERE WAS I?
OH YEAH... THE CHICK TOOK OFF.
ONE OUT OF TWO AIN'T BAD.

SO YOU HAD TO KICK ME IN THE BACK, HUH?
WHAT ARE YOU COMPLAINING ABOUT... WE'RE STILL ALIVE, AREN'T WE?
FAIR ENOUGH.
SAY, DID YOU CATCH THE PART ABOUT JUNGLE JANE THERE BEING HIRED BY SOMEONE TO TAKE YOU OUT?
YEAH, STORY OF MY LIFE. WHAT'S YOUR POINT?
I SAY WE FOLLOW HER TRAIL.
WELL LET'S GET BUSY, WE'RE LOSING DAYLIGHT.

BASED ON THE SURROUNDING TOPOGRAPHY AND VISIBLE LANDMARKS, I'D ESTIMATE THAT THE WOMAN IS HEADED UPSTREAM.
MOST LIKELY TOWARD THE PEAK OF THE-
YEAH, OKAY.
SO. YOU'RE A *PIRATE*, RIGHT? SAIL THE FIVE SEAS AND ALL THAT?
ACTUALLY, THERE ARE *SEVEN* SEAS.
AND NO- I'M A *POLICE DETECTIVE* NOW.
SURE, YOU JUST KEEP TELLIN' YOURSELF THAT THERE, OFFICER FRIENDLY. YOU'RE ABOUT AS MUCH OF A *POLICE* DETECTIVE AS I AM A *LIBRARIAN* DETECTIVE.
I'VE NEVER SEEN A *BEAT COP* RUN A MAN THROUGH WITHOUT EVEN *FLINCHING*. IT TAKES A KILLER TO KNOW A KILLER, EDDIE...
...YOU AND I ARE CUT FROM THE SAME CLOTH.
IT WASN'T *ALWAYS* THAT WAY.
A LONG TIME AGO THERE WAS A BOY WHO REALLY *DID* WANT NOTHING MORE THAN TO BE A COP...

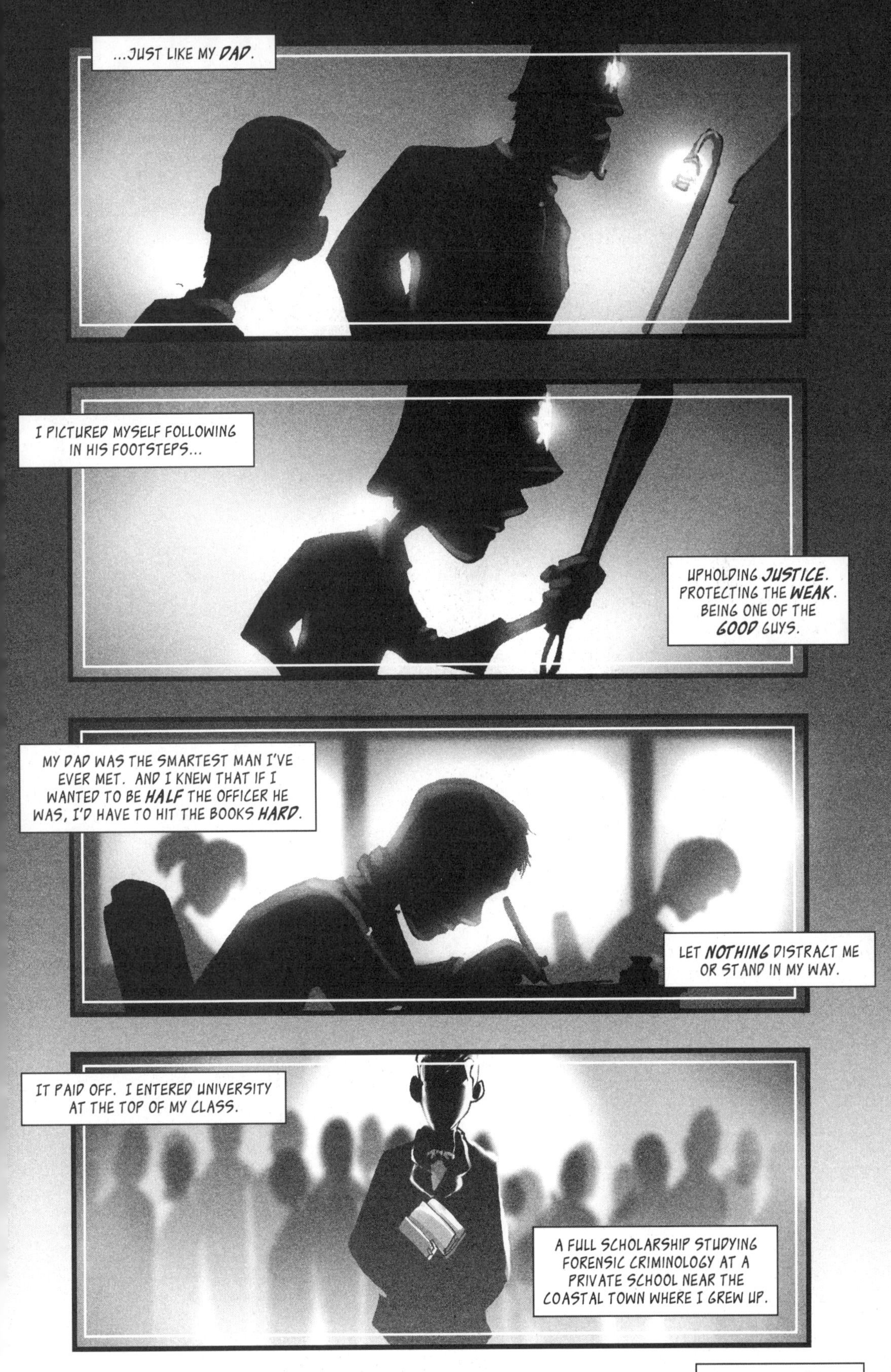
...JUST LIKE MY DAD.
I PICTURED MYSELF FOLLOWING IN HIS FOOTSTEPS...
UPHOLDING JUSTICE. PROTECTING THE WEAK. BEING ONE OF THE GOOD GUYS.
MY DAD WAS THE SMARTEST MAN I'VE EVER MET. AND I KNEW THAT IF I WANTED TO BE HALF THE OFFICER HE WAS, I'D HAVE TO HIT THE BOOKS HARD.
LET NOTHING DISTRACT ME OR STAND IN MY WAY.
IT PAID OFF. I ENTERED UNIVERSITY AT THE TOP OF MY CLASS.
A FULL SCHOLARSHIP STUDYING FORENSIC CRIMINOLOGY AT A PRIVATE SCHOOL NEAR THE COASTAL TOWN WHERE I GREW UP.
LIFE WAS PERFECT.

THAT IS, UNTIL THE BLACKSHIPS ARRIVED.
THEY CAME AT DAWN AND WERE UPON US BEFORE WE REALIZED WHAT WAS HAPPENING.
THE POLICE - MY FATHER INCLUDED - WERE THE FIRST TO RESPOND TO THE ATTACK.
THEY WERE ALSO THE FIRST TO DIE.
SOMETIMES, I THINK MAYBE THEY WERE THE FORTUNATE ONES.
THOSE THAT WEREN'T SLAIN THE FIRST DAY GOT TO DIE SLOWLY AND PAINFULLY OVER THE WEEKS TO COME.
THEN THERE WERE US LUCKY FEW.
WE GOT TO GO ON A LITTLE BOAT RIDE.
AWAY FROM THAT TOWN. AWAY FROM THAT LIFE.
AWAY FROM EVERYTHING SANE IN THIS WORLD.

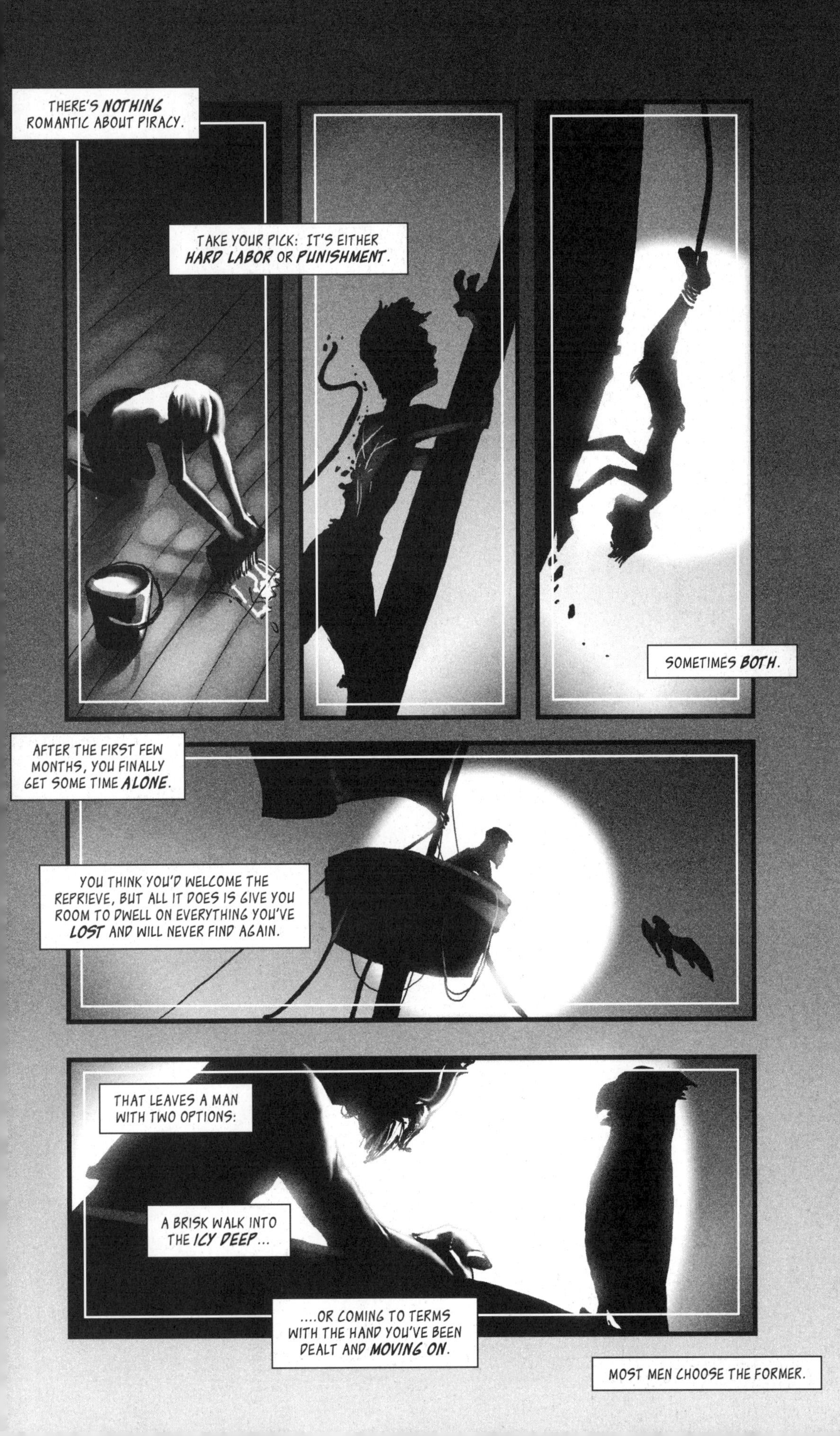
THERE'S NOTHING ROMANTIC ABOUT PIRACY.
TAKE YOUR PICK: IT'S EITHER HARD LABOR OR PUNISHMENT.
SOMETIMES BOTH.
AFTER THE FIRST FEW MONTHS, YOU FINALLY GET SOME TIME ALONE.
YOU THINK YOU'D WELCOME THE REPRIEVE, BUT ALL IT DOES IS GIVE YOU ROOM TO DWELL ON EVERYTHING YOU'VE LOST AND WILL NEVER FIND AGAIN.
THAT LEAVES A MAN WITH TWO OPTIONS:
A BRISK WALK INTO THE ICY DEEP...
....OR COMING TO TERMS WITH THE HAND YOU'VE BEEN DEALT AND MOVING ON.
MOST MEN CHOOSE THE FORMER.

I HATE TO INTERRUPT YOUR SOB STORY THERE... AND DON'T GET ME WRONG - I UNDERSTAND THE NEED FOR A GOOD CRY ONCE IN A WHILE... BUT DO YOU GOT ANY IDEA WHERE WE ARE?
I SWEAR THIS IS THE THIRD TIME WE'VE PASSED THAT FALLEN TREE.
YOU THINK THIS JUNGLE'S ONLY GOT ROOM FOR ONE FALLEN TREE? DON'T WORRY, WE'RE STILL ON HER TRAIL.
WHAT, YOU PICK UP HER SCENT WITH THAT BLOODHOUND NOSE OF YOURS?
GO ON BOY, SNIFF HER OUT... WHERE SHE AT?
HAVE YOU EVER ACTUALLY TRACKED ANYONE, MISTER HOTSHOT DETECTIVE?
I'M NOT REALLY SURE SHE COULD MAKE IT ANY EASIER FOR US TO FOLLOW HER - WHAT WITH ALL THE BROKEN BRANCHES. NOT TO MENTION THE BLOOD TRAIL.
YEAH OKAY. SO... WHAT, YOU WANT LIKE A MERIT BADGE OR SOMETHING NOW? YOU DO YOUR THING, I'LL DO MINE.

I GOTTA SAY, YOU'RE NOT EXACTLY WINNING ME OVER WITH THIS WHOLE "PIRACY" THING.
YOU DON'T MAKE IT SOUND TOO APPEALING.
IN THE BEGINNING, IT'S NOT. BEING PRESS GANGED ISN'T EXACTLY LIKE JOINING A JUG BAND.
THAT WAS TOO BAD. I PLAY A MEAN WASHBOARD.
YOU GUYS REALLY BURY TREASURE ALL OVER THE PLACE? WHAT'S THAT ALL ABOUT?
SURE, I'VE BURIED MY FAIR SHARE OF LUCRE.
IT'S NOT EXACTLY LIKE YOU CAN SAIL DOWN TO THE OL' SAVINGS AND LOAN AND OPEN A CHECKING ACCOUNT, IF YOU KNOW WHAT I MEAN.
YEAH. YOU EVER GET THAT SCURVY THING?
AYE. AIN'T AS BAD AS THEY MAKE IT SOUND.
YOU EVER KEEL HAUL A MAN?
HOW ABOUT I JUST FINISH MY STORY.
I DIDN'T HAVE THE HEART TO TELL THE POOR GUY I DIDN'T REALLY CARE. HE JUST LOOKED SO SAD WITH HIS BIG PUPPY DOG EYES.

AFTER YOU'VE BEEN IN IT A WHILE, YOU START TO GET A TASTE OF THE GLORY.
IT'S DECEPTIVE, BUT SIMPLE:
FIRST YOU FIND THE MAPS THAT LEAD TO THE TREASURE.
NEXT YOU FIND THE TREASURE ITSELF.
THEN THE TREASURE FINDS SOME THINGS FOR YOU.
AND PRETTY SOON THE CYCLE STARTS ALL OVER AGAIN.

IT DOESN'T MATTER HOW GOOD A CAPTAIN YOU ARE...
THE PURSUIT OF ALL THOSE RICHES INEVITABLY LEADS TO MUTINY.
AND MUTINY WILL SOMETIMES LEAD TO LESS-THAN-DESIRABLE LEADERSHIP.
POOR CAPTAINS, IN TURN, LEAD TO ALL KINDS OF HARDSHIP.
AND THERE'S ONLY ONE CURE FOR A POOR CAPTAIN:
MORE MUTINY.
SENSE A PATTERN HERE?

IT TOOK TEN LONG YEARS, AND ME BECOMING A CAPTAIN MYSELF, BEFORE I COULD SEE THAT PATTERN WITH MY OWN EYES.
IT WASN'T A QUESTION OF *IF* I'D FIND A CUTLASS IN MY BACK. IT WAS *WHEN*.
AND THAT'S WHERE I DECIDED IT WAS TIME TO CAST MY *OWN* ANCHOR.
AND I'VE BEEN ON THIS ISLAND EVER SINCE.
TRYING TO CHART A COURSE BACK THROUGH THE FOG TO A LIFE THAT HAS SOME MEANING.

AWWW, HAPPILY EVER AFTER. HOW SWEET.
YOU GET SOME GLASS SLIPPERS OUTTA THAT DEAL, TOO?
LISTEN SAM. I'VE KNOWN YOU FOR WHAT, FORTY-EIGHT HOURS? I CAN ALREADY TELL THAT YOU TREAT EVERYONE THIS WAY.
THERE MUST BE SOME MAJOR INSECURITIES AT PLAY FOR YOU TO BE SUCH AN ASS ALL THE TIME.
TIME OUT THERE, HOSS. YOU'RE NOT MY PSYCHO-THERAPIST. I AIN'T PAYIN' YOU BY THE HOUR. IF I WANNA HEAR YOUR LIFE STORY, I'LL ASK FOR IT.
YOU'VE BEEN ASKING QUESTIONS AND LISTENING FOR THE LAST TWO HOURS. I GUESS I ASSUMED YOU WERE INTERESTED.
I WAS FEIGNING INTEREST. IT MADE YOU FEEL BETTER, DIDN'T IT?
SEE... I'M A NICE GUY AFTER ALL.
WE DIDN'T COME ALL THE WAY OUT HERE TO BICKER.
BESIDES, I'VE LOST THE BLOOD TRAIL. OUR PREY SEEMS TO HAVE ELUDED US.
THAT'S BECAUSE YOU'VE BECOME THE PREY!

I APPRECIATE THAT YOU TWO FOLLOWED ME THIS FAR. IT'LL MAKE KILLING YOU ALL THAT MUCH EASIER.
SWEETIE, FROM WHERE I'M STANDIN' IT LOOKS LIKE YOU'RE ABOUT TWO PINTS LOW.
WE'RE HERE FOR THE REST.
YOUR RHINOCEROS IS DEAD AND YOU HAVE NO WEAPON. WE'LL GUT YOU FROM STEM TO STERN.
GO GET 'EM, AHAB.
WHAT THE TWO OF YOU DON'T REALIZE IS THAT THESE HALLOWED GROUNDS ARE A PLACE OF POWER.
A SOURCE OF ANCIENT STRENGTH.

HOW EXACTLY DOES A MUSTY OLD GRAVEYARD GIVE A CRAZY JUNGLE LADY WITH NO RHINO ANY KIND OF POWER?
SHE DIDN'T SAY IT GAVE HER POWER.
AND THAT'S WHEN THE TALKING MIME SHOWED UP.
I ALWAYS LOVE IT WHEN THEY DO THAT "I'M STUCK IN A GLASS BOX" THING.
OR THE "PRETENDING TO WALK DOWN STAIRS" GAG. THAT'S A GOOD ONE, TOO.
IF I'D HAD MY WITS ABOUT ME, I WOULD'VE ASKED HIM TO SHOW ME HOW IT'S DONE.
BUT I WAS TOO BUSY BLACKIN' OUT.
SNEAKY MIME MAGIC.

REST WHILE YOU CAN, SAM NOIR, FOR YOU ARE MINE NOW.
TO BE CONTINUED...

I REALLY MEAN IT, SNUGGLEBUG...
DRINKING YOUR COFFEE IS LIKE DRINKING ANGELS' TEARS.
IT'S THE BEST, BEST, BEST, BEST, EVER.
OH, SAM. YOU BIG SILLYHEAD. YOU SAY THAT EVERY MORNING.
AND I MEAN IT EVERY MORNING, JASMINE.
ISN'T THAT RIGHT, KIDS?
YES, DADDY!!!
WE LOVE YOU!

DADDY, COME OUTSIDE! WE MADE YOU SOMETHING.
REEEALLY, SWEETIE? WHAT IS IT?
IT'S A SURPRISE!
WELL, I CAN'T VERY WELL TURN DOWN A GIFT FROM THE FIFTEEN BEST KIDS IN THE WHOLE WIDE WORLD.
IT'S PERFECT! HOW DID YOU KNOW?!?
WE ALWAYS KNOW WHAT MAKES OUR SAMMY-BEAR HAPPY.
DADDY, DADDY, DO YOU LIKE IT?
HERE LIES
SAM NOIR.
HE DIED ALONE
FATHER OF NONE

NONE?
BUT I'VE GOT FIFTEEN OF THE MOST WONDERFUL...
NO YOU DON'T, SAM.
YOU KILLED ALL OF US.
JASMINE, NO!

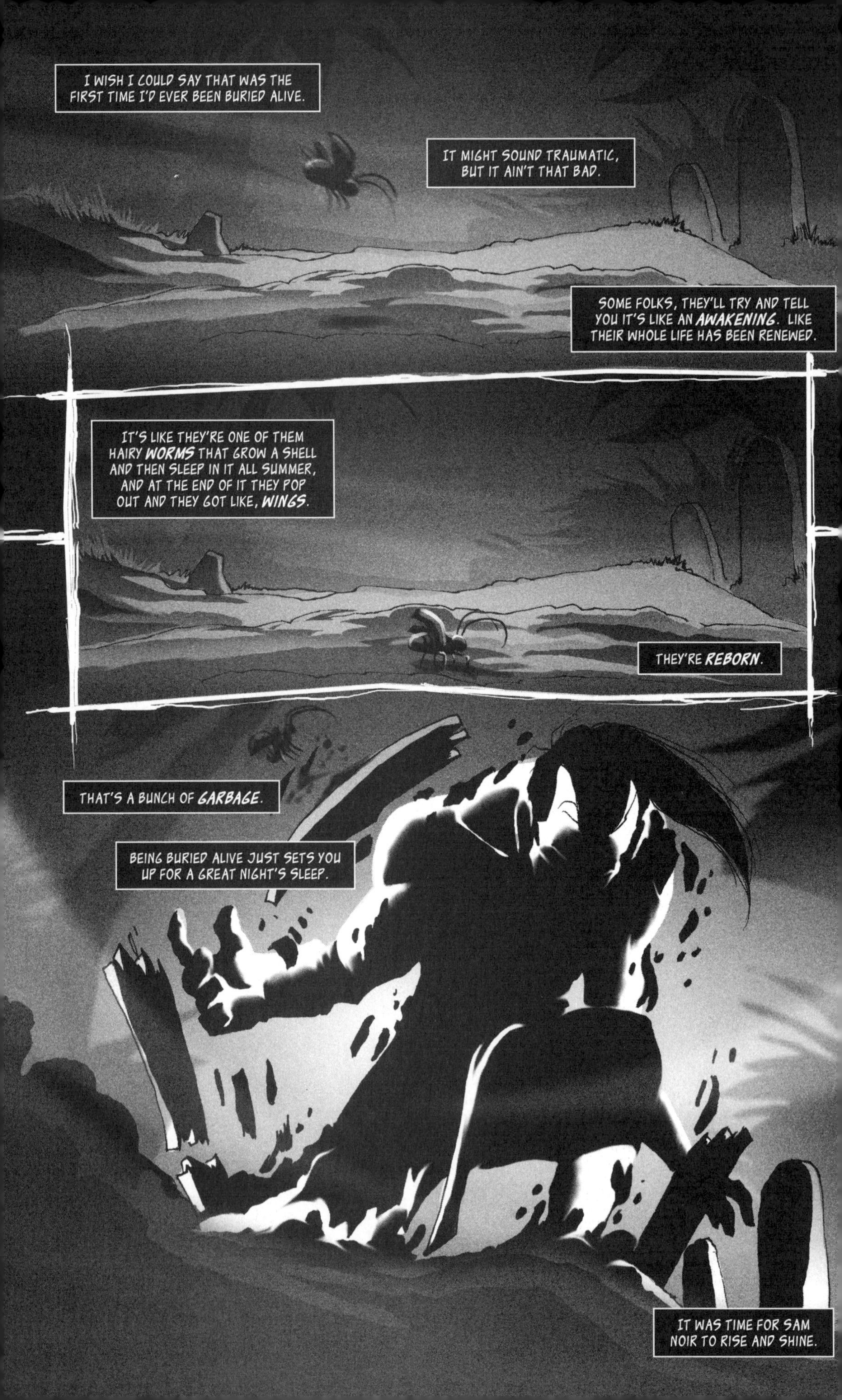
I WISH I COULD SAY THAT WAS THE FIRST TIME I'D EVER BEEN BURIED ALIVE.
IT MIGHT SOUND TRAUMATIC, BUT IT AIN'T THAT BAD.
SOME FOLKS, THEY'LL TRY AND TELL YOU IT'S LIKE AN AWAKENING. LIKE THEIR WHOLE LIFE HAS BEEN RENEWED.
IT'S LIKE THEY'RE ONE OF THEM HAIRY WORMS THAT GROW A SHELL AND THEN SLEEP IN IT ALL SUMMER, AND AT THE END OF IT THEY POP OUT AND THEY GOT LIKE, WINGS.
THEY'RE REBORN.
THAT'S A BUNCH OF GARBAGE.
BEING BURIED ALIVE JUST SETS YOU UP FOR A GREAT NIGHT'S SLEEP.
IT WAS TIME FOR SAM NOIR TO RISE AND SHINE.

TWO EMPTY GRAVES. LOOKED LIKE EDDIE WAS AN EARLY RISER.
MUST BE ALL THAT OCEAN LIVING.
CA-CAW!
HEY POLLY. WHERE'S YOUR MASTER AT?
RRAAWWWK.
YEAH, THANKS FOR THE TIP.
BIRD WASN'T MUCH HELP.
...NOT THE PLAN...
...CONTRACT SAYS...
...CAN'T BACK OUT NOW...
SCREW THE BIRD. I COULD HEAR JUNGLE JANE RUNNING HER MOUTH OFF SOMEWHERE CLOSE.

FIGURED I'D GO TAKE A LOOK.
WE HAD AN ARRANGEMENT, YOU BACKWATER, TWO-BIT MYSTIC.
WE SHOULD HAVE KILLED SAM WHEN WE HAD THE CHANCE INSTEAD OF BURYING HIM IN THE GROUND LIKE A TURNIP.
AS I RECALL, YOU HAD PLENTY OF OPPORTUNITY TO KILL THE MAN BEFORE YOU CAME LIMPING BACK HERE WITH YOUR TAIL BETWEEN YOUR LEGS.
BESIDES, BURYING SAM NOIR HAS BENEFITS FAR BEYOND ANY PETTY TRINKETS OUR EMPLOYER MAY OFFER ME.
I WAS PRETTY EXCITED TO SEE THAT CHATTY MIME AGAIN. HE AND I HAD SOME UNFINISHED BUSINESS.
SPEAKING OF REUNIONS, THAT'S WHEN I SPOTTED MY TWO GOOD BUDDIES: CHOPPY AND CUT-CUT.
I COULD TELL THEY WERE HAPPY TO SEE ME.

TRINKETS?!?
IF WE FOLLOW THROUGH ON THIS CONTRACT, WE'LL BE REWARDED WITH MORE RICHES THAN EITHER YOU OR I COULD'VE EVER DREAMED OF.
YOU'RE AFRAID OF HIM, AREN'T YOU?
OUR EMPLOYER? HELL YES, I'M TERRIFIED OF THE MAN.
YOU WERE THERE. YOU HEARD WHAT HE SAID WOULD HAPPEN TO US IF WE FAILED.
YES, I'M FULLY AWARE OF THE CONSEQUENCES. BUT I FEAR NO MAN.
LIFE AND DEATH ARE JUST FORCES TO BE CONTROLLED BY MY WILL, AND OUR EMPLOYER WILL LEARN THAT SOON ENOUGH.
SO NOT ONLY ARE YOU ROBBING ME OF MY JUST REWARDS, BUT YOU'RE RECKLESSLY ENDANGERING BOTH OF OUR LIVES ALL FOR SOME EGOMANIACAL POWER TRIP?
I'M SORRY THAT YOU CANNOT SEE THE TRUE POTENTIAL OF MY ACTIONS.

THAT'S WHEN EDDIE CAME STROLLIN' OUT OF THE WOODS.

I'D UNDERESTIMATED HIM.

IT WAS **SHOWTIME**, AND HE WAS MAKING HIS MOVE.

AND IT WAS MY KIND OF MOVE, TOO.
KUDOS, EDDIE.
ONE DOWN, ONE TO GO.
IT LOOKED LIKE EDDIE WAS ABOUT TO GET THE DROP ON THE MIME AS WELL.
FIGURED IT WAS TIME FOR ME TO GET IN ON SOME OF THAT ACTION.

ALL ABOARD THE SAMURAI EXPRESS!
FIRST STOP: SWORDSVILLE.
SECOND STOP: KILLINGSBURG.
CHOO. CHOO.

THANKS FOR THE DIRTNAP, DOC.
BUT I THINK IT'S ABOUT TIME WE PUT **YOU** IN THE GROUND.
I'M SAD TO SEE THAT YOU HAVE MORE WILLPOWER THAN I GAVE YOU CREDIT FOR.
IT SEEMS I'LL HAVE TO SETTLE FOR A **CONSOLATION PRIZE**.
THAT'S TOO BAD, CUZ WE'RE ALL OUTTA **CUPIE DOLLS** AT **THIS** CARNIVAL.
EDDIE, YOU WANT THIS ONE, OR SHOULD I TAKE HIM?
EDDIE?
ED?

AWW, HELL.

NOT *AGAIN*.

AND I WAS JUST STARTIN' TO *LIKE* THE GUY.

AS YOU CAN SEE, YOUR FRIEND WAS **MUCH** EASIER TO TURN THAN YOURSELF.
IT WAS MY DESIRE TO HAVE YOU **BOTH** AS MY ZOMBI SERVANTS, BUT AT LEAST NOW I CAN CLAIM THAT REWARD AFTER ALL.
EDMUND GROG, **I COMMAND YOU!**
KILL SAM NOIR!

I HAVE TO GIVE THE MAN CREDIT. WHEN EDDIE GETS RILED UP, HE'S ONE HECK OF A FIGHTER.
HE'S FAST LIKE A BARRACUDA RIDING A GAZELLE.
AND THAT'S SUPER FAST.
BUT THE THING IS...

I DON'T MEAN TO BOAST...
..BUT I'M FAST LIKE A CHEETAH RIDING A BOLT OF LIGHTNING.
YOU DON'T EVEN KNOW I'M GONNA STRIKE UNTIL YOU'VE GOT FOUR FANGS IN YOUR NECK...
...AND A MILLION VOLTS RUNNIN' DOWN YOUR SPINE.
...HE AIN'T NO SAMURAI.

LISTEN EDDIE, YOU BEEN A REAL STAND-UP GUY THE LAST COUPLE OF DAYS...
BUT I ALWAYS KNEW IT'D COME TO THIS.
CA-CAW!

POLLY GOT THERE JUST IN TIME.
HE MUST HATE MIMES EVEN MORE THAN *ME*...
...BECAUSE HE TOOK THAT SUCKER *OUT*.
THAT BIRD WAS *HARD CORE*.
HE WAS GETTIN' A *BIG* OL' HELPING OF EYEBALL SALAD.
WHATEVER POLLY DID, IT WORKED.
EDDIE WENT DOWN LIKE A SACK OF POTATOES.

EYES ON ME, BUDDY. POP QUIZ.
HOW MANY SWORDS AM I HOLDIN' UP?
YOU BASTARD.
OH, RIGHT. I FORGOT. YOU'RE BLIND.
THAT'S OKAY. YOU'LL JUST HAVE TO TAKE THE QUIZ IN BRAILLE.
THE CORRECT ANSWER WAS "TWO".

UP AND AT 'EM, SWABBIE.
TIME TO GET YOUR SEA LEGS BACK.
WHAT THE HELL *HAPPENED*?
THE LAST THING I REMEMBER, SOME VOODOO *WITCH DOCTOR* SHOWED UP AND EVERYTHING WENT BLACK.
YEAH, YOU CRIED LIKE A LITTLE BABY.
DON'T WORRY THOUGH, I TOOK CARE OF *EVERYTHING*. I'LL FILL YOU IN LATER.
I TOLD HIM ALL ABOUT IT.
ALL EXCEPT FOR THE PART WHERE I ALMOST HAD TO *KILL* HIM. THAT'S JUST BETWEEN ME AND *YOU*, HONEY...

...DON'T TELL HIM I TOLD YOU.
YOU'RE SUCH A NICE YOUNG MAN.
THANK YOU MA'AM. I TRY.
YOU REMIND ME OF MY CAT, *SNIFFLES*.
YEAH, I GET THAT A LOT.
I HOPE I'M NOT INTERRUPTING... SAM, CAN WE TALK FOR A MINUTE?
SURE, WE WERE JUST CHATTING ABOUT CATS.

YOU DIDN'T NEED TO COME ALONG, YOU KNOW.
I DO JUST FINE ON MY OWN.
I'M SURE YOU DO, BUT I OWE YOU MY LIFE.
AND MORE IMPORTANTLY THAN THAT, YOU MADE ME REALIZE THAT I WAS LIVING A LIE.
I CAN'T PRETEND TO BE SOMETHING I'M NOT.
DON'T MAKE ME REGRET SAVIN' YOUR ASS BY GETTING ALL WEEPY ON ME.
THIS AIN'T NO FIELD TRIP. WHERE WE'RE HEADED, YOU'RE GOING TO NEED TO BE TOUGH AS NAILS.
YOU'RE CERTAIN YOU KNOW WHERE THIS GUY IS?
THE CONTRACT WE PULLED OFF THE JUNGLE WOMAN HAD ALL THE DETAILS.
AND YOU SAY YOU'VE DEALT WITH HIM BEFORE?
OH YEAH, WE'VE MET...

...I MADE A PROMISE TO HIM THAT I INTEND TO *KEEP*.
Fuyu
I THOUGHT I'D KILLED THE PERSON WHO TOOK JASMINE AWAY FROM ME.
NOW I WASN'T SO SURE.
BUT I WAS GONNA FIND OUT.
THE END.

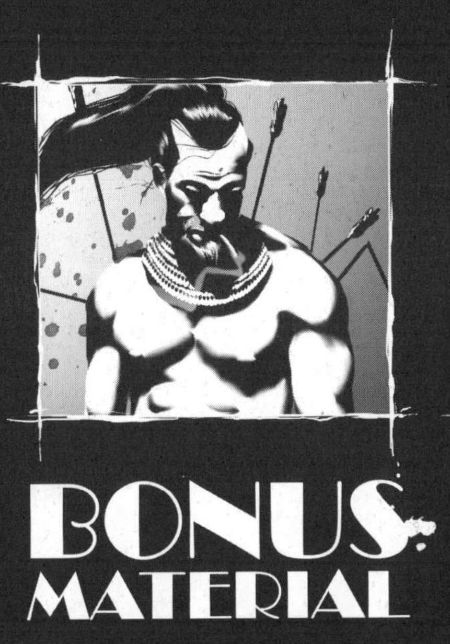

BONUS MATERIAL

Cover for issue one of Samurai Detective.

Cover for issue two of Samurai Detective.

Cover for issue three of Samurai Detective.

Cover for collected special edition of Samurai Detective.

Cover for issue one of Ronin Holiday.

Cover for issue two of Ronin Holiday.

Cover for issue three of Ronin Holiday.

Pin-up by Jimmie Robinson

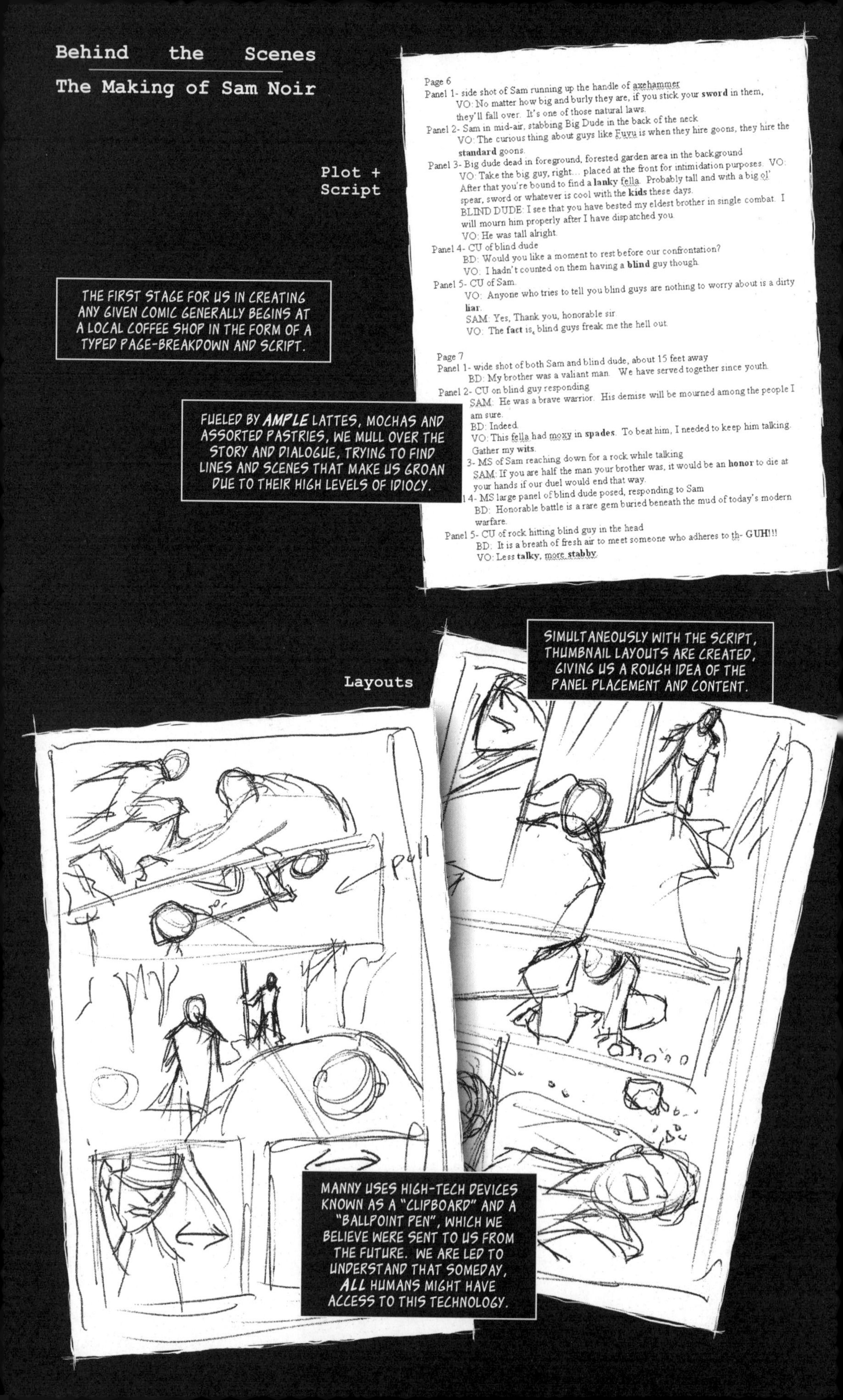

Page 6
Panel 1- side shot of Sam running up the handle of axehammer
VO: No matter how big and burly they are, if you stick your **sword** in them, they'll fall over. It's one of those natural laws.
Panel 2- Sam in mid-air, stabbing Big Dude in the back of the neck
VO: The curious thing about guys like Fuyu is when they hire goons, they hire the **standard** goons.
Panel 3- Big dude dead in foreground, forested garden area in the background
VO: Take the big guy, right… placed at the front for intimidation purposes. VO: After that you're bound to find a **lanky** fella. Probably tall and with a big ol' spear, sword or whatever is cool with the **kids** these days.
BLIND DUDE: I see that you have bested my eldest brother in single combat. I will mourn him properly after I have dispatched you.
VO: He was tall alright.
Panel 4- CU of blind dude
BD: Would you like a moment to rest before our confrontation?
VO: I hadn't counted on them having a **blind** guy though.
Panel 5- CU of Sam.
VO: Anyone who tries to tell you blind guys are nothing to worry about is a dirty **liar**.
SAM: Yes, Thank you, honorable sir.
VO: The **fact** is, blind guys freak me the hell out.

Page 7
Panel 1- wide shot of both Sam and blind dude, about 15 feet away
BD: My brother was a valiant man. We have served together since youth.
Panel 2- CU on blind guy responding
SAM: He was a brave warrior. His demise will be mourned among the people I am sure.
BD: Indeed.
VO: This fella had moxy in **spades**. To beat him, I needed to keep him talking. Gather my **wits**.
3- MS of Sam reaching down for a rock while talking
SAM: If you are half the man your brother was, it would be an **honor** to die at your hands if our duel would end that way.
l 4- MS large panel of blind dude posed, responding to Sam
BD: Honorable battle is a rare gem buried beneath the mud of today's modern warfare.
Panel 5- CU of rock hitting blind guy in the head
BD: It is a breath of fresh air to meet someone who adheres to th- **GUH!!!**
VO: Less **talky**, more **stabby**.

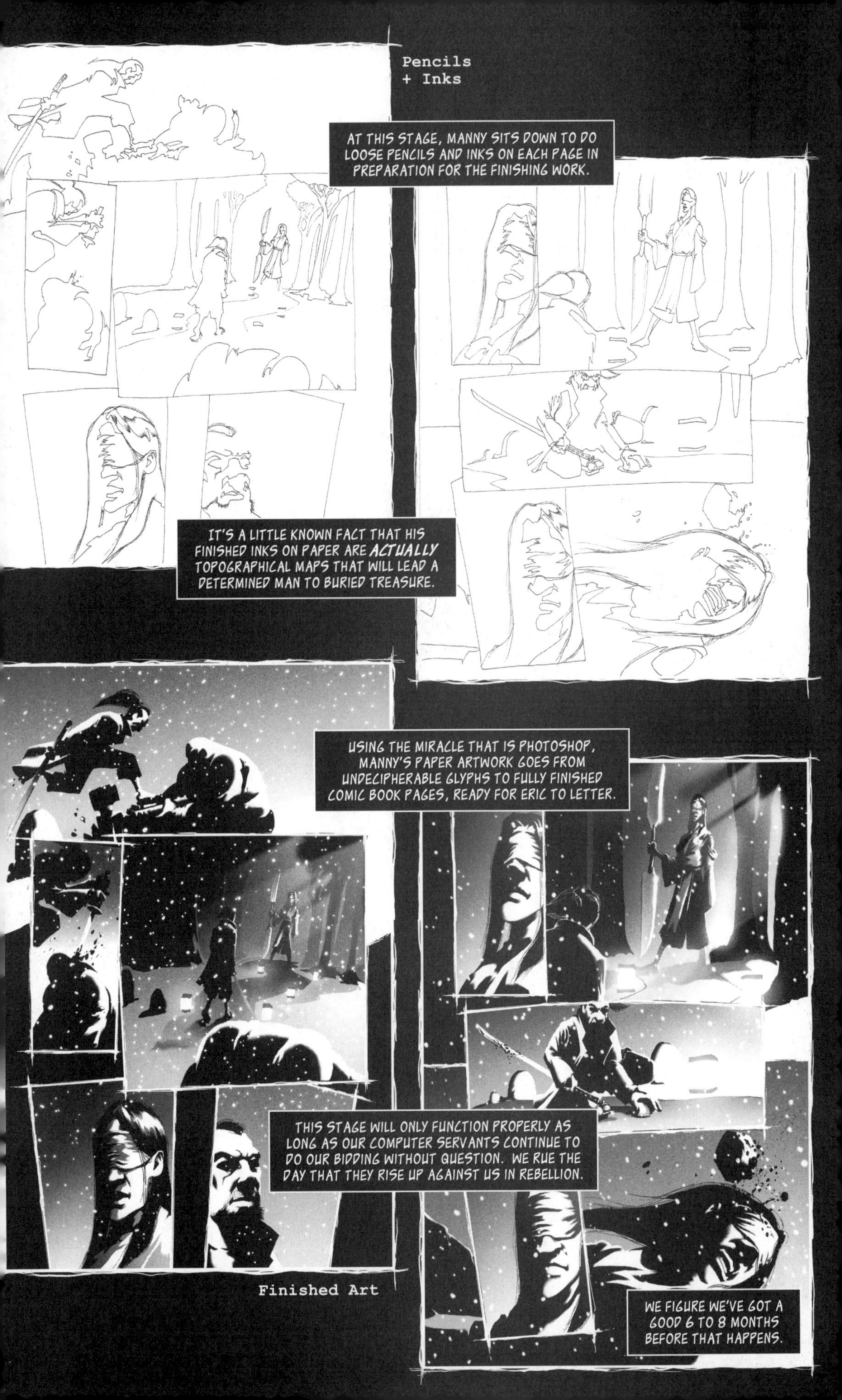
Pencils
+ Inks
AT THIS STAGE, MANNY SITS DOWN TO DO LOOSE PENCILS AND INKS ON EACH PAGE IN PREPARATION FOR THE FINISHING WORK.
IT'S A LITTLE KNOWN FACT THAT HIS FINISHED INKS ON PAPER ARE ACTUALLY TOPOGRAPHICAL MAPS THAT WILL LEAD A DETERMINED MAN TO BURIED TREASURE.
USING THE MIRACLE THAT IS PHOTOSHOP, MANNY'S PAPER ARTWORK GOES FROM UNDECIPHERABLE GLYPHS TO FULLY FINISHED COMIC BOOK PAGES, READY FOR ERIC TO LETTER.
THIS STAGE WILL ONLY FUNCTION PROPERLY AS LONG AS OUR COMPUTER SERVANTS CONTINUE TO DO OUR BIDDING WITHOUT QUESTION. WE RUE THE DAY THAT THEY RISE UP AGAINST US IN REBELLION.
Finished Art
WE FIGURE WE'VE GOT A GOOD 6 TO 8 MONTHS BEFORE THAT HAPPENS.

Pin-up by Seth Damoose

Concept art for Sam Noir.

Cover created for the submission package.

Character concept art for Akina.

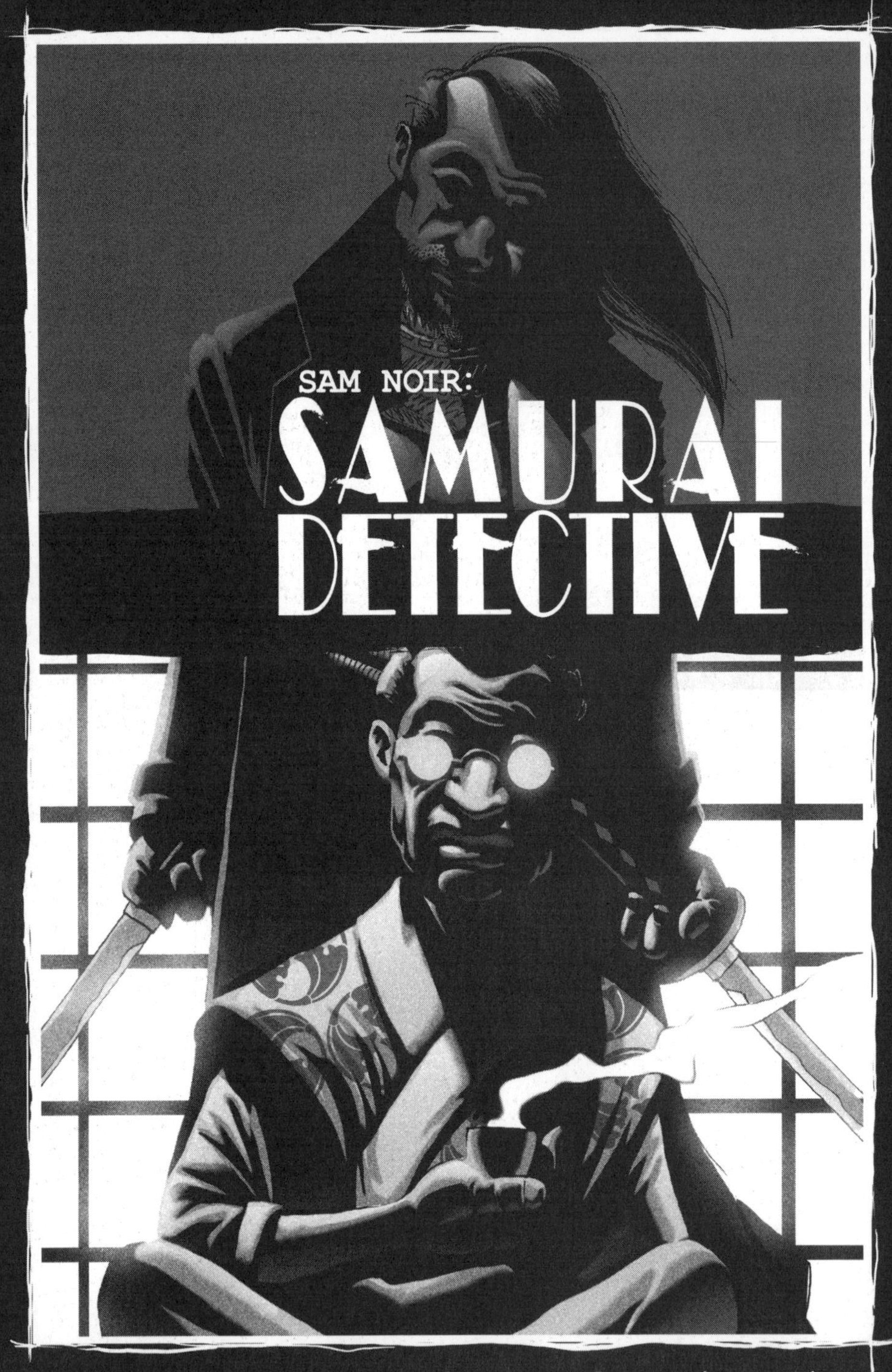

Unused cover for issue two of Samurai Detective.

Another unused cover for issue two of Samurai Detective.

Inked stage for unused concept cover.

Unused concept cover.

Concept art for Eddie Grog.

Unused concept promotional piece.